# Earth Science Experiments

# FACTS ON FILE SCIENCE EXPERIMENTS

# Earth Science Experiments

Pamela Walker
Elaine Wood

An imprint of Infobase Publishing

**Earth Science Experiments**

Facts On File, Inc.
An imprint of Infobase Publishing
132 West 31st Street
New York NY 10001

**Library of Congress Cataloging-in-Publication Data**
Walker, Pam, 1958-
Earth science experiments / Pamela Walker, Elaine Wood.
p. cm. — (Facts on File science experiments)
Includes bibliographical references and index.
ISBN 978-0-8160-8170-7
1. Earth sciences–Experiments–Juvenile literature. I. Wood, Elaine,
1950- II. Title.
QE29.W27 2011
550.78–dc22
2010042985

Facts On File books are available at special discounts when purchased in bulk quantities for businesses, associations, institutions, or sales promotions. Please call our Special Sales Department in New York at (212) 967-8800 or (800) 322-8755.

You can find Facts On File on the World Wide Web at http://www.factsonfile.com

All links and Web addresses were checked and verified to be correct at the time of publication. Because of the dynamic nature of the Web, some addresses and links may have changed since publication and may no longer be valid.

Editor: Frank K. Darmstadt
Copy Editor: Betsy Feist at A Good Thing, Inc.
Project Coordinator: Aaron Richman
Art Director: Howard Petlack
Production: Victoria Kessler
Illustrations: Hadel Studios
Cover printed by: Bang Printing, Brainerd, MN
Book printed and bound by Bang Printing, Brainerd, MN
Date printed: December 2010
Printed in the United States of America

10 9 8 7 6 5 4 3 2 1

This book is printed on acid-free paper.

# Contents

Preface ......................................................................... vii

Acknowledgments ............................................................. xi

Introduction ................................................................... xiii

Safety Precautions ........................................................... xvii

1. Planimetric Maps ..........................................................1

2. Topographic Maps .........................................................8

3. Crystal Growth and Size ...............................................14

4. Erosion by Soil Type ....................................................21

5. Mineral Identification ..................................................27

6. Soil Color and Temperature ..........................................34

7. Slope Stability ...........................................................42

8. Erosion on Sand Dunes ...............................................49

9. Naming Rocks ...........................................................55

10. Rock Deformation .....................................................62

11. Half-life in Rock Dating ..............................................70

12. Wind Chill ...............................................................77

13. Relative Humidity .....................................................84

14. Tracking a Hurricane ..................................................91

15. Hailstone Formation ..................................................99

16. Speed of Evaporation ...............................................105

17. Color Filters on Telescopes ........................................113

18. Making a Planisphere ...............................................119

19. Using a Planisphere ..................................................126

20. History of Astronomy ................................................133

Scope and Sequence Chart ............................................. 142

Grade Level .................................................................. 144

Setting ....................................................................... 145

**Our Findings** .......................................................................... 147

**Glossary** ............................................................................... 161

**Internet Resources** ............................................................... 166

**Periodic Table of Elements** .................................................... 169

**Index** .................................................................................. 170

# Preface

For centuries, humans have studied and explored the natural world around them. The ever-growing body of knowledge resulting from these efforts is science. Information gained through science is passed from one generation to the next through an array of educational programs. One of the primary goals of every science education program is to help young people develop critical-thinking and problem-solving skills that they can use throughout their lives.

Science education is unique in academics in that it not only conveys facts and skills; it also cultivates curiosity and creativity. For this reason, science is an active process that cannot be fully conveyed by passive teaching techniques. The question for educators has always been, "What is the best way to teach science?" There is no simple answer to this question, but studies in education provide useful insights.

Research indicates that students need to be actively involved in science, learning it through experience. Science students are encouraged to go far beyond the textbook and to ask questions, consider novel ideas, form their own predictions, develop experiments or procedures, collect information, record results, analyze findings, and use a variety of resources to expand knowledge. In other words, students cannot just hear science; they must also do science.

"Doing" science means performing experiments. In the science curriculum, experiments play a number of educational roles. In some cases, hands-on activities serve as hooks to engage students and introduce new topics. For example, a discrepant event used as an introductory experiment encourages questions and inspires students to seek the answers behind their findings. Classroom investigations can also help expand information that was previously introduced or cement new knowledge. According to neuroscience, experiments and other types of hands-on learning help transfer new learning from short-term into long-term memory.

Facts On File Science Experiments is a multivolume set of experiments that helps engage students and enable them to "do" science. The high-interest experiments in these books put students' minds into gear and give them opportunities to become involved, to think independently, and to build on their own base of science knowledge.

As a resource, Facts On File Science Experiments provides teachers with new and innovative classroom investigations that are presented in a clear, easy-to-understand style. The areas of study in this multivolume set include forensic science, environmental science, computer research, physical science, weather and climate, space and astronomy and many others. Experiments are supported by colorful figures and line illustrations that help hold students' attention and explain information. All of the experiments in these books use multiple science process skills such as observing, measuring, classifying, analyzing, and predicting. In addition, some of the experiments require students to practice inquiry science by setting up and carrying out their own open-ended experiments.

Each volume of the set contains 20 new experiments as well as extensive safety guidelines, glossary, correlation to the National Science Education Standards, scope and sequence, and an annotated list of Internet resources. An introduction that presents background information begins each investigation to provide an overview of the topic. Every experiment also includes relevant specific safety tips along with materials list, procedure, analysis questions, explanation of the experiment, connections to real life, and an annotated further reading section for extended research.

Pam Walker and Elaine Wood, the authors of Facts On File Science Experiments, are sensitive to the needs of both science teachers and students. The writing team has more than 40 years of combined science teaching experience. Both are actively involved in planning and improving science curricula in their home state, Georgia, where Pam was the 2007 Teacher of the Year. Walker and Wood are master teachers who hold specialist degrees in science and science education. They are the authors of dozens of books for middle and high school science teachers and students.

Facts On File Science Experiments, by Walker and Wood, facilitates science instruction by making it easy for teachers to incorporate experimentation. During experiments, students reap benefits that are not available in other types of instruction. One of these benefits is the opportunity to take advantage of the learning provided by social interactions. Experiments are usually carried out in small groups, enabling students to brainstorm and learn from each other. The validity of group work as an effective learning tool is supported by research in neuroscience, which shows that the brain is a social organ and that communication and collaboration are activities that naturally enhance learning.

Experimentation addresses many different types of learning, including lateral thinking, multiple intelligences, and constructivism. In lateral thinking, students solve problems using nontraditional methods. Long-established, rigid procedures for problem-solving are replaced by original ideas from students.

When encouraged to think laterally, students are more likely to come up with unique ideas that are not usually found in the traditional classroom. This type of thinking requires students to construct meaning from an activity and to think like scientists.

Another benefit of experimentation is that it accommodates students' multiple intelligences. According to the theory of multiple intelligences, students possess many different aptitudes, but in varying degrees. Some of these forms of intelligence include linguistic, musical, logical-mathematical, spatial, kinesthetic, intrapersonal, and interpersonal. Learning is more likely to be acquired and retained when more than one sense is involved. During an experiment, students of all intellectual types find roles in which they can excel.

Students in the science classroom become involved in active learning, constructing new ideas based on their current knowledge and their experimental findings. The constructivist theory of learning encourages students to discover principles for and by themselves. Through problem solving and independent thinking, students build on what they know, moving forward in a manner that makes learning real and lasting.

Active, experimental learning makes connections between newly acquired information and the real world, a world that includes jobs. In the 21st century, employers expect their employees to identify and solve problems for themselves. Therefore, today's students, workers of the near future, will be required to use higher-level thinking skills. Experience with science experiments provides potential workers with the ability and confidence to be problem solvers.

The goal of Walker and Wood in this multivolume set is to provide experiments that hook and hold the interest of students, teach basic concepts of science, and help students develop their critical-thinking skills. When fully immersed in an experiment, students can experience those "Aha!" moments, the special times when new information merges with what is already known and understanding breaks through. On these occasions, real and lasting learning takes place. The authors hope that this set of books helps bring more "Aha" moments into every science class.

# Acknowledgments

This book would not exist were it not for our editor, Frank K. Darmstadt, who conceived and directed the project. Frank supervised the material closely, editing and making invaluable comments along the way. Betsy Feist of A Good Thing, Inc., is responsible for transforming our raw material into a polished and grammatically correct manuscript that makes us proud.

# Introduction

Earth science is one of the most basic fields of study because it focuses on our planet and its role in the universe. Through this science, we can become knowledgeable about the planet we call home, the source of our food, the atmosphere that surrounds us, the water we drink, and our neighbors in space.

*Earth Science Experiments* is one volume in Facts On File Science Experiments, a new multivolume set of books on various fields of science. The goal of this volume is to provide science teachers with 20 original experiments that convey basic principles of Earth science. The activities in *Earth Science Experiments* are designed to help students understand that the Earth systems directly affect us, and that we impinge on the Earth systems by activities that put pressure on natural resources, stress the atmosphere, and damage the water supply. Each experiment in the book is a proven classroom activity that broadens understandings of both scientific facts and the nature of science. The investigations are appropriate for both middle and high school classes.

To accommodate different modes of learning, activities in *Earth Science Experiments* vary in style. Some are inquiry experiments that ask students to develop a hypothesis, come up with a procedure and materials list, collect data, and draw conclusions. Other experiments follow the traditional format of providing directions for students. In several experiments, students develop models or manipulatives to help them understand and work with difficult abstract concepts. Some of the experiments cover one class period, while others extend over several days. Regardless of their approach, all the activities are engaging, hooking the interest of students and connecting to prior knowledge so that learning is real and meaningful.

The study of Earth science has many practical applications, making it a topic to which students can relate. It enables us to locate and develop valuable mineral and petroleum resources. Through Earth science, we learn more about how humans are affecting their environment. As a result, we can develop methods of helping the planet recover from damage done in the past and present as well as protecting it from future harm.

In addition, Earth science plays a day-to-day role in our lives in predicting weather and forecasting dangerous weather events.

The field of Earth science is made up of several branches, including geology, meteorology, and astronomy. Geology, the primary Earth science, focuses on the materials that make up Earth and the processes carried out on the planet. In the geology section of this book, two experiments acquaint students with a fundamental skill: map reading. "Planimetric Maps" focuses on reading and constructing two-dimensional maps. Students expand their skills in "Topographic Maps," an experiment that enables them to understand the construction of three-dimensional maps.

"Crystal Growth and Size" examines the conditions that affect the dimensions of crystals and relates crystal growth to natural and commercial events. "Erosion by Soil Type" looks at one of the most common problems in land management, loss of soil by wind and water. This is an inquiry experiment in which students evaluate some of the variables that relate to erosion and consider how soil loss might be prevented. In "Slope Stability," students learn how to calculate the slope of a landform, then carry out a partial inquiry to determine how one variable, such as soil composition or moisture content, influences soil's resistance to a change in position. In "Erosion on Sand Dunes," students investigate saltation and study the science behind the effectiveness of different types of windscreens found on dunes.

The characteristics of minerals, rocks, and soil are topics of several experiments. In "Mineral Identification," students differentiate types of minerals and relate techniques of classification to careers in locating minerals resources. "Naming Rocks" demonstrates some simple field tests that geologists use to identify rocks. Once students have mastered the tests, they use them to make a field guide for identifying unknown rocks. To find out how color impacts soil's ability to absorb energy, students design and carry out an inquiry investigation in "Soil Color and Temperature."

To expand their knowledge of the history of Earth's crust, students conduct two activities that relate to changes in rock materials. "Rock Deformation" lets students model the behavior of rocks under stress, then create three-dimensional models of folded rock layers. In "Half-Life in Rock Dating," students use the fictitious elements beanium and lentilium to demonstrate how the decay of radioactive compounds into stable daughter elements can be used to determine the age of a rock.

On a daily basis, people interact with meteorologists to plan their activities. Meteorology studies the conditions of the atmosphere and determines how changes in the atmosphere affect weather and climate. The experiments in this volume focus on some of the basics of meteorology. "Wind Chill" measures heat loss and calculates how wind changes perception of temperature. In "Relative Humidity," students make a psychrometer from a small milk carton and use the device to measure relative humidity on the school campus. In "Tracking a Hurricane," students examine data on the changing atmospheric conditions of Hurricane Katrina and track the path of the storm across the Gulf of Mexico and into Louisiana. "Hailstorm Formation" helps students discover the factors that must be in place for the formation of hailstones. "Speed of Evaporation" is an inquiry experiment in which students find out how one factor, either heat, light, or wind, affects rate of evaporation.

Astronomy, the study of universe, may be the most mysterious and fascinating branch of Earth science. Although objects in space seem remote, students learn that they have a tremendous influence on life on Earth. In the astronomy section of this book, students examine objects through color filters to see how they improve analysis of telescopic images in "Color Filters on Telescopes." To enhance stargazing, students construct a personal sky map that can be used to locate constellations in "Making a Planisphere." In the experiment, "Using a Planisphere," students set the sky maps to the current date and time and use them to observe the night sky. "History of Astronomy" is a research project in which students find out how the body of knowledge that comprises the science of astronomy today has been built on the work of earlier scientists.

Earth is our home and understanding what is happening on it is essential to its protection. Through Earth science, we can take care of the environment and predict how our current activities might affect the future. Since today's students are the future stewards of our planet, the authors hope that this book will help them see the value of Earth science as a tool in sustainable development and management of our resources.

# Safety Precautions

## REVIEW BEFORE STARTING ANY EXPERIMENT

Each experiment includes special safety precautions that are relevant to that particular project. These do not include all the basic safety precautions that are necessary whenever you are working on a scientific experiment. For this reason, it is absolutely necessary that you read and remain mindful of the General Safety Precautions that follow. Experimental science can be dangerous and good laboratory procedure always includes following basic safety rules. Things can happen quickly while you are performing an experiment—for example, materials can spill, break, or even catch on fire. There will not be time after the fact to protect yourself. Always prepare for unexpected dangers by following the basic safety guidelines during the entire experiment, whether or not something seems dangerous to you at a given moment.

We have been quite sparing in prescribing safety precautions for the individual experiments. For one reason, we want you to take very seriously the safety precautions that are printed in this book. If you see it written here, you can be sure that it is here because it is absolutely critical.

Read the safety precautions here and at the beginning of each experiment before performing each lab activity. It is difficult to remember a long set of general rules. By rereading these general precautions every time you set up an experiment, you will be reminding yourself that lab safety is critically important. In addition, use your good judgment and pay close attention when performing potentially dangerous procedures. Just because the book does not say "Be careful with hot liquids" or "Don't cut yourself with a knife" does not mean that you can be careless when boiling water or using a knife to punch holes in plastic bottles. Notes in the text are special precautions to which you must pay special attention.

## GENERAL SAFETY PRECAUTIONS

Accidents can be caused by carelessness, haste, or insufficient knowledge. By practicing safety procedures and being alert while conducting experiments, you can avoid taking an unnecessary risk. Be sure to check the individual experiments in this book for additional safety regulations and adult supervision requirements. If you will be working in a laboratory, do not work alone. When you are working off site, keep in groups with a minimum of three students per group, and follow school rules and state legal requirements for the number of supervisors required. Ask an adult supervisor with basic training in first aid to carry a small first-aid kit. Make sure everyone knows where this person will be during the experiment.

## PREPARING

- Clear all surfaces before beginning experiments.
- Read the entire experiment before you start.
- Know the hazards of the experiments and anticipate dangers.

## PROTECTING YOURSELF

- Follow the directions step by step.
- Perform only one experiment at a time.
- Locate exits, fire blanket and extinguisher, master gas and electricity shut-offs, eyewash, and first-aid kit.
- Make sure there is adequate ventilation.
- Do not participate in horseplay.
- Do not wear open-toed shoes.
- Keep floor and workspace neat, clean, and dry.
- Clean up spills immediately.
- If glassware breaks, do not clean it up by yourself; ask for teacher assistance.
- Tie back long hair.
- Never eat, drink, or smoke in the laboratory or workspace.
- Do not eat or drink any substances tested unless expressly permitted to do so by a knowledgeable adult.

## USING EQUIPMENT WITH CARE

- Set up apparatus far from the edge of the desk.
- Use knives or other sharp, pointed instruments with care.

- Pull plugs, not cords, when removing electrical plugs.
- Clean glassware before and after use.
- Check glassware for scratches, cracks, and sharp edges.
- Let your teacher know about broken glassware immediately.
- Do not use reflected sunlight to illuminate your microscope.
- Do not touch metal conductors.
- Take care when working with any form of electricity.
- Use alcohol-filled thermometers, not mercury-filled thermometers.

## USING CHEMICALS

- Never taste or inhale chemicals.
- Label all bottles and apparatus containing chemicals.
- Read labels carefully.
- Avoid chemical contact with skin and eyes (wear safety glasses or goggles, lab apron, and gloves).
- Do not touch chemical solutions.
- Wash hands before and after using solutions.
- Wipe up spills thoroughly.

## HEATING SUBSTANCES

- Wear safety glasses or goggles, apron, and gloves when heating materials.
- Keep your face away from test tubes and beakers.
- When heating substances in a test tube, avoid pointing the top of the test tube toward other people.
- Use test tubes, beakers, and other glassware made of Pyrex™ glass.
- Never leave apparatus unattended.
- Use safety tongs and heat-resistant gloves.
- If your laboratory does not have heatproof workbenches, put your Bunsen burner on a heatproof mat before lighting it.
- Take care when lighting your Bunsen burner; light it with the airhole closed and use a Bunsen burner lighter rather than wooden matches.

- Turn off hot plates, Bunsen burners, and gas when you are done.
- Keep flammable substances away from flames and other sources of heat.
- Have a fire extinguisher on hand.

## FINISHING UP

- Thoroughly clean your work area and any glassware used.
- Wash your hands.
- Be careful not to return chemicals or contaminated reagents to the wrong containers.
- Do not dispose of materials in the sink unless instructed to do so.
- Clean up all residues and put in proper containers for disposal.
- Dispose of all chemicals according to all local, state, and federal laws.

## BE SAFETY CONSCIOUS AT ALL TIMES!

# 1. Planimetric Maps

## Topic

A planimetric map provides the information needed to travel from one location to another.

## Introduction

If you are taking a trip to a place you have never visited, how will you get there? Unless you have a global positioning system (GPS) device, you will most likely rely on a *map*, a diagram that represents a region of Earth's surface. Maps can be designed for specific purposes, such as showing the locations of national forest, the positions of types of rocks, or regions of a water table. A traveler would most likely use a specific type of planimetric map, a road map that provides locations of towns, roads, and major geographic features.

On a large planimetric map, you can see lines of *latitude* and *longitude* (see Figure 1). These are imaginary lines that are part of the global grid system. The positions of these lines can be used as points of reference so that one can specify a location exactly. Latitude lines run around the globe. The *equator* is an imaginary line that runs east and west around the middle of Earth an equidistance from the north and south poles. Other east-west lines of latitude run parallel to the equator. The equator is assigned a position of zero degrees (0°), and there are 90° of arc between the equator and each pole. These measurements reflect the fact that if you were to draw a line from the Earth's center to the north pole, the angle would be 90° above the horizon. The same type of measurement shows that the latitude of the south pole is 90° south (90°S). The numbers represent angles measured from the center of the Earth. Each angle is described in three components: degrees, minutes, and seconds. A degree is 60 minutes (60') of arc, and a minute is 60 seconds (60") of arc. So a location can be pinpointed using all three, such as 42° 15' 8" or as decimal units of degrees.

Lines of longitude (*meridians*) run from pole to pole, each one passing through the equator. Since the equator is a circle, it can be divided into 360°. For reference purposes, one meridian was selected as 0°. This line

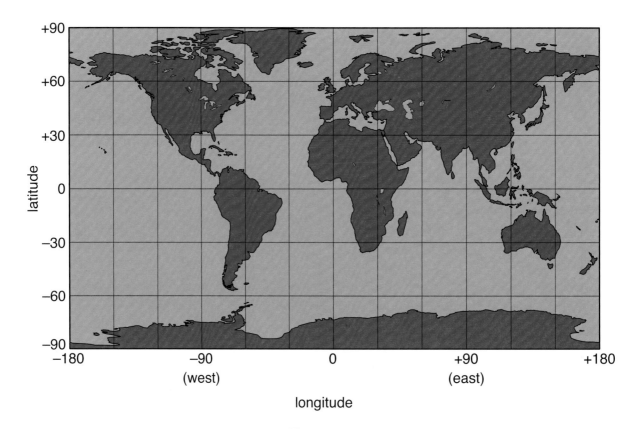

**Figure 1**

**Planimetric map with lines of latitude and longitude**

runs through Greenwich, England, and is known as the *prime meridian*. The other meridians are described as lines east or west of the prime meridian.

In this activity, you will read a planimetric map of the United States, using latitude and longitude for reference. You will also make a planimetric map that other students can use.

## Time Required

30 minutes for Part A
45 minutes for Part B

## Materials

- compass
- computer with access to the Internet
- tape measure
- world map
- science notebook

| Safety Note | When working outside the school building to design or use a map, stay within the areas prescribed by your teacher. Please review and follow the safety guidelines at the beginning of this volume. |

## Procedure, Part A

1. Examine the map of the continental United States in Figure 2.

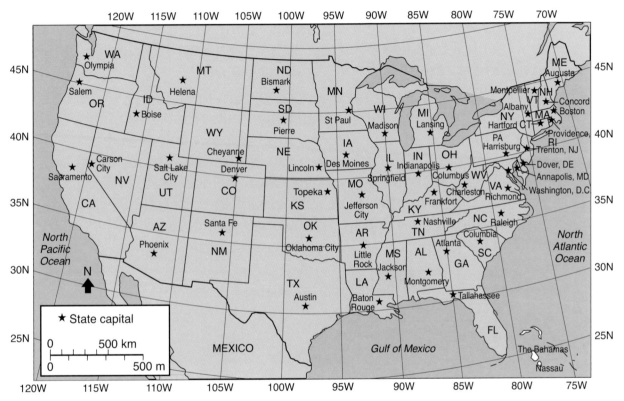

**Figure 2**

2. Notice that the grid (latitude and longitude) lines that are closest to Denver, Colorado, are 40°N and 105°W. If this map also showed minutes and degrees, you could see that Denver's exact location is 39° 44' 21" N and 104° 59' 3" W.

3. Use the map to determine the grid lines that are closest to the following cities: Boise, Idaho; Montgomery, Alabama; Raleigh, North Carolina; Oklahoma City, Oklahoma; and Sacramento, California. Answer Analysis question 1.

4. Compare your findings to the exact latitudes and longitudes coordinates using the iTouchMap.com Web site at http://itouchmap.com/latlong.html, an online resource that enables you to touch a point on the map to find its exact latitude and longitude.

5. Answer Analysis question 2.

## Procedure, Part B

1.  Working with a group, draw a map that shows how to get to some destination, such as a building, a monument, or a flower bed, near your school. Base the map on your group's collective knowledge of the area. Mark the point that is the destination with an X. As you are working, draw the map as accurately as possible. Keep in mind that your map should have a *scale*, which indicates relative distance. For example, a distance of 10 meters (m) could be represented on the map by a line of 1 centimeter (cm), or 10 feet (ft) could be represented by a line of one inch. You can see an example of the scale in the lower left-hand corner of Figure 2.

2.  Include symbols, such as the ones shown in Figure 3, on your map for special features such as buildings, hills, roads, or paths. Give your map a *legend*, an explanation of the symbols. Make sure your legend includes a north arrow. Draw the arrow without using any instruments or help from your teacher. Include any other legend features that will make your map easier to understand. You can see an example of a legend in the lower left-hand corner of Figure 2, which shows that a "★" is used to show state capitals.

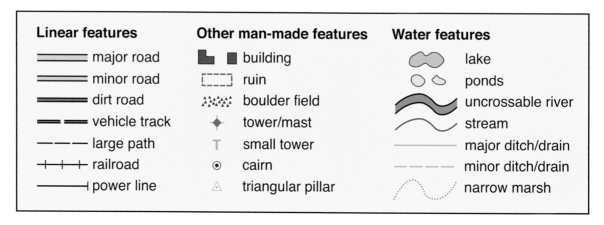

**Figure 3**

3.  Check the accuracy of your map. To do so:

    a.  Go to the destination that you mapped and use a tape measure to measure the distances. Make corrections to your map based on these measurements.

    b.  Use a compass to determine which direction is north. If necessary, correct your arrow on your map.

    c.  Add any map symbols that are needed.

4.  Exchange maps with another group.

5. Use the other group's map to find the point marked X.

6. Return to the classroom and meet with the group with whom you exchanged maps. Discuss the good and bad points of each group's map. Make changes or corrections as needed.

7. Answer Analysis questions 3 through 7.


## Analysis

1. According to the map in Figure 2, what are the latitude and longitude lines closest to these cities? (a) Boise, Idaho; (b) Montgomery, Alabama; (c) Raleigh, North Carolina; (d) Oklahoma City, Oklahoma; and (e) Sacramento, California.

2. According to the map in Figure 2, what are the latitude and longitude lines closest to the city or area where you live? Using iTouchMap, what are the exact coordinates of your city or area?

3. Using the legend in the bottom left-hand corner of the map in Figure 2, how many miles is it from Sacramento, California, to New York City?

4. How far is it from Tallahassee, Florida, to Nassau, the Bahamas?

5. What is the scale on the map your group created?

6. When your group checked the accuracy of your map, what kinds of changes did you have to make?

7. Why are legends on maps important?


## What's Going On?

Have you ever given directions to someone who was lost? If so, you probably used reference points and landmarks in your directions. You may have said "Travel two blocks down this street and turn right at the gas station." Giving directions to people is like providing them with a mental map.

Maps are essential tools for finding new locations on land. In the experiment, you gained experience in both using and making written maps. By using a map, you achieved insight into the relationship of your current location to the place you want to go. You probably discovered that landmarks provide invaluable assistance in describing a location. Your map included a scale, most likely with a bar that has tick marks to represent distance. Some maps have verbal scales, statements such as, "One inch equal 100 miles." Others have a representative fraction, written as a ratio such as 1:100. The numerator of the fraction represents units on the map and the denominator units on the ground. In the example 1:100, one unit (such as feet or meters) on the map represents 100 units on the ground.

## Connections

*Cartography*, the art and science of map making, is a very old discipline. Cartographers try to represent the surface of Earth and its features as accurately as possible. The maps they produce are a product of the knowledge of the time and the interest of the map maker. The oldest known maps are clay tablets created by the Babylonians about 2300 B.C.E. Greek and Roman cartographers advanced the science and drew or painted maps showing that the Earth is a sphere about 350 B.C.E. Mathematical science was applied to map making when the Greek scientist Eratosthenes (275–195 B.C.E.) calculated the Earth's circumference.

In medieval times, most maps were symbolic rather than scientific and showed the world as one landmass surrounded by seas. Religious ideas dominated European maps, which showed Jerusalem in the center. During the same time, Arabian mapmakers produced more accurate diagrams that convey true relationships of distance and position. Maps of any type were rare commodities, and only individuals of wealth or high rank possessed them. With the invention of the printing press in the 15th century, maps became more available and therefore more useful. The first world map that showed the continents we recognize today was created by German cartographer Martin Waldseemüller (ca. 1417–ca. 1520) in 1507, it showed the Americas as relatively thin strips of land in the west. Over the next three centuries, maps were refined as explorers and scientists gained information. However, some regions were relatively unknown until aerial photography was available after World War I.

## Want to Know More?

See appendix for Our Findings.

## Further Reading

David Rumsey Map Collection. Available online. URL: http://www. davidrumsey.com/. Accessed September 25, 2010. This historical map collection provides more than 22,000 images with information about each.

Hebert, John R. "The Map That Named America, Library Acquires 1507 Waldseemüller Map of the World." Library of Congress. Available online. URL: http://www.loc.gov/loc/lcib/0309/maps.html. Accessed September 25, 2010. This article shows a photograph of Waldseemüller's original map and explains how it was acquired by the Library of Congress.

Krygier, John. "Making Maps: DIY Cartography," August 13, 2009. Available online. URL: http://makingmaps.net/. Accessed September 25, 2010. This Web site for the advanced student, associated with the book *Making Maps* by Krygier and Denis Wood, discusses the problems and challenges of present-day cartography.

# 2. Topographic Maps

## Topic

Topographic maps show the relief of a region.

## Introduction

You have probably used maps to help you find your way to another city. Maps showing roads, towns, and cities are two dimensional. A different type of map provides a third dimension, *elevation*. Known as a *topographic map*, this type of diagram shows *relief*, or variations in elevation of Earth's surface or the difference between the highest point, such as a mountain top and the lowest point.

On every topographic map, elevation is measured as the vertical distance above or below sea level. To understand how elevation is shown on a map, imagine that you can view an island from the side. On this imaginary island, you have measured the elevation and drawn a line around the island at 10, 20, 30, and 40 feet (ft) (3, 6, 9, and 12 meters [m]) and so forth. Your drawing might look something like Figure 1a. If you could see the island from above, the lines you drew would look like Figure 1b.

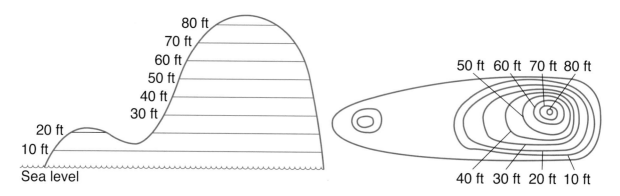

a. Sideview of island          b. Topographical map of island

**Figure 1**

**Measuring and representing elevation**

A topographic map resembles Figure 1b. Lines drawn across a topographic map connect points of equal elevation. Each line, which represents a plane above sea level, is a *contour line*. Contour lines make it possible to evaluate the height of a mountain or steepness of a slope using a map. Contour lines are separated by intervals of equal elevation. For example, the contour interval of a map showing little change in elevation could be 5 ft (1.5 m). A steep or rugged terrain might have a contour interval of 500 ft (152 m). The interval is given in the map *legend*, an area that explains the symbols on the map. The legend also indicates the scale of the map and contains a north-pointing arrow.

Once you understand the rules of contour mapping, you are ready to read the map. Lines that are very close together indicate steep slopes, while those far apart show gentle inclines. Some lines may be *hachured*, indicating a decrease rather than an increase in elevation. Contour lines bend or point upstream when crossing a river or stream. All waters flow down slopes, so bent lines are one way to determine direction of stream flow. In this activity, you will examine a topographic map, then use your map-reading skills to make two topographic maps.

## Time Required

55 minutes

## Materials

- colored pencils
- photocopy of Figure 3
- science notebook

**Safety Note**    Please review and follow the safety guidelines at the beginning of this volume.

## Procedure

1. Examine the contour map in Figure 2.
2. Answer Analysis questions 1 through 6.

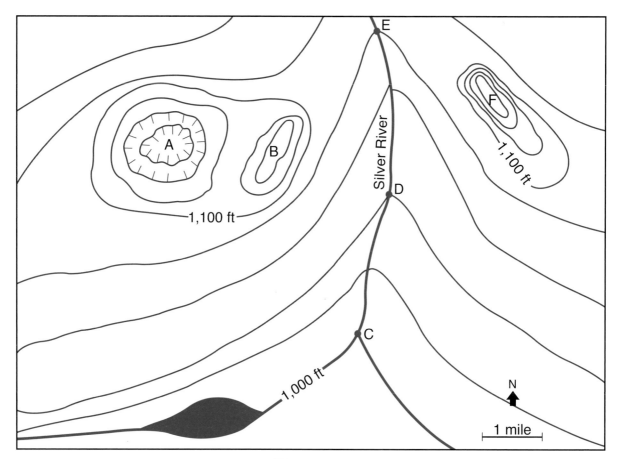

**Figure 2**

**Contour map**

3. Examine the map in Figure 3, which include measures of elevations.

4. On a photocopy of the map, add the contour lines. The contour interval on this map is 10 ft (3 m). Notice that not all contour measurements are given in even numbers. For example, one measurement is 11 ft and another is 9 ft. You should draw the contour lines for 10 ft between these two measurements. Some lines have been drawn for you.

5. Answer Analysis questions 7 through 9.

6. In your science notebook, draw a topographic map of an imaginary region. Be creative and artistic with your map. Your topographic may can show any features that you like, but must include the following: (a) one or more tall hills or mountains; (b) steep hill; (c) gentle slope; (d) waterway; (e) depression; (f) N-pointing arrow; (g) legend.

   Use these colors on your map: brown—contour lines; red—roadways; blue—shoreline, creek (narrow line), pond, river (wide line); gray—buildings.

**7.** Answer Analysis questions 10 through 12.

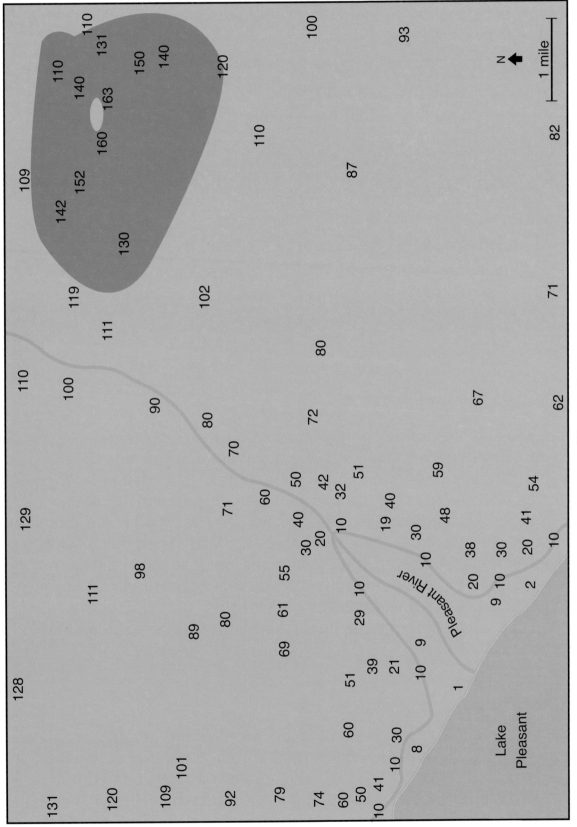

Figure 3

## Analysis

1. The contour interval on the map in Figure 2 is 20 ft. What is the highest elevation on the map? What is the lowest elevation? What is the relief of the map?
2. What is the elevation at point A? point B?
3. What is the elevation at point D?
4. How much higher is point E than point C?
5. On which side is mountain F the steepest: north or south? How do you know?
6. In which direction does Silver River flow?
7. What is the relief on the map in Figure 3?
8. In which direction is Pleasant River flowing?
9. Where is the greatest area of relief (steepest slope) on this map?
10. How did you indicate a depression on your topographic map?
11. What is the relief on your topographic map?
12. What is the contour interval on your map?

## What's Going On?

Before you can begin a topographic map, you must know the elevations of exact locations on map. Once the elevations are determined, contour lines can be added. Other features can be indicated as needed with symbols. *Cartographers*, specialists who make maps, find elevations in one of two ways: field surveys or aerial photographs. Field surveys require the use of elevation-measuring instruments on location, so they can be expensive. Aerial photographs are commonly used because they are less expensive. An aerial team takes thousands of pictures that overlap slightly. Once the pictures are developed, they are examined with a *stereoscope*, an instrument that enables one to read the photographs for elevation and distance.

## Connections

In the summer of 2009, NASA and Japan released the newest, most extensive topographic map of the world between 83°N and 83°S. The digital map was made from 1.3 million stereoscope images that were taken with the Japanese instrument, the Advanced Spaceborne Thermal Emission and Reflection Radiometer (Aster), aboard the U.S. satellite

*Terra*. Aster, one of several instruments on *Terra* that observes Earth, gathers images in the range of visible light through infrared energy of the electromagnetic spectrum. The new map is an improvement over older version, especially in regions of deserts and steep inclines. Because the data on this new topographic map is very accurate, it will be useful to scientists in fields such as engineering, environmental management, and energy exploration. In addition, the data will have practical application with city planners, fire fighters, and public works designers.

## Want to Know More?

See appendix for Our Findings.

## Further Reading

NASA. Aster Imagery. Available online. URL: http://www.nasa.gov/topics/earth/features/20090629.html. Accessed September 25, 2010. This Web site shows some of the images taken by Aster.

NOAA, National Geophysical Data Center. "U.S. State Images from 30 Second Topographic Data," 3rd ed. June 1999. Available online. URL: http://www.ngdc.noaa.gov/mgg/topo/state.html. Accessed September 25, 2010. By clicking on the name of a state, one can view and analyze a topographic map of the area.

Topographic Maps, 2010. Available online. URL: http://www.forgefx.com/casestudies/prenticehall/ph/topo/topo.htm. Accessed September 25, 2010. This interactive, three-dimensional map simulation lets you make changes to a landscape and see how those changes affect a topographic map of the area.

U.S. Geographical Survey. "Topographic Map Symbols," February 25, 2005. Available online. URL: http://egsc.usgs.gov/isb/pubs/booklets/symbols/moreinformation.html. Accessed September 25, 2010. This Web site provides links to topographic maps and information on how to read maps.

# 3. Crystal Growth and Size

## Topic

Contaminants can affect the rate of growth and size of mineral crystals.

## Introduction

A *crystal* is a solid substance that has a defined, repeating atomic structure. The minimal group of elements that form the basis of a crystal is called the *unit cell*. Each unit cell contains all the parts of the crystal structure; if repeated, the unit would allow you to build the entire crystal. You can think of a unit cell as a children's toy block, a perfect cube, which is duplicated and stacked in all directions. While there are millions of different crystals, there are only seven lattice systems into which all unit cells can be classified.

The names of the seven lattice systems are the *cubic, hexagonal, trigonal, tetragonal, orthorhombic, monoclinic,* and *triclinic*. Each one is defined by the relationship of the sides (a, b, c) and angles ($\alpha$, $\beta$, $\gamma$) of the repeating unit (see Figure 1). There are only seven lattice systems because there are only seven three-dimensional shapes that *tessellate*, or fill in the space with regular *polyhedra* so that the edges and faces meet with no overlap or gaps. The cubic lattice system is the most symmetric. In it, $a = b = c$ and $\alpha = \beta = \gamma = 90°$. Moving along the list from hexagonal to triclinic, the lattice systems become less and less symmetric. For instance, in the trigonal system $a = b = c$ and $\alpha = \beta = \gamma$, but the angles are not right angles. If we continue losing symmetry elements, we eventually reach the triclinic system in which $a \neq b \neq c$ and $\alpha \neq \beta \neq \gamma \neq 90°$.

The crystallization of a substance (elements, compounds, or groups of compounds) depends on several conditions including time, solvent, temperature, evaporation rate, and presence of contaminants. Some compounds easily crystallize, such as NaCl or table salt, a cubic lattice system, or $C_{12}H_{22}O_{11}$ or sucrose, a monoclinic system, while others do not. For example a great deal of research effort is spent on attempts to crystallize proteins, but to date of the millions of proteins known, crystal structures of only about 50,000 have been reported. The right conditions for crystal growth depend on the type of compound or element that is crystallizing, and different conditions can lead to different crystal shapes and sizes or to no crystals at all. In this experiment you will determine the best method of growing sugar crystals.

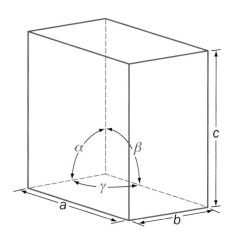

**Figure 1**

**In this unit cell of a primitive monoclinic lattice, side a = side b = side c and the angles α = β = γ = 90°**

## Time Required

20 minutes on day 1
15 minutes a day on days 2 through 6
30 minutes on day 7

## Materials

- sugar
- food coloring
- corn syrup
- 2 mason jars (that have been washed and are very clean)
- water (enough to use from 1/2 to 1 cup in each jar)
- 2 pencils
- tape

- 2 bamboo skewers or 2 precut pieces of string, about 8 inches (in) (20 centimeters [cm])
- 2 clothespins (if skewers are used)
- 2 metal washers (if string is used)
- ruler
- microscope (optional)
- electronic balance
- science notebook

**Safety Note** **Please review and follow the safety guidelines at the beginning of this volume.**

## Procedure

1. Prepare the crystallizing surface.
    a. Start with two pieces of string that have been cut to the same length or two bamboo skewers that are the same length.
    b. Wet the two strings or two skewers and coat them with sugar (table sugar or larger-grained coarse sugar work well for this). Allow the surfaces to dry.
    c. If you are using string, attach a metal washer to one end to act as a weight. Tie the other end of each string to the middle of a pencil (see Figure 2). If you use wooden skewers, use a clothes pen to attach each one to a pencil.
2. Prepare the crystallizing solution by dissolving sugar in boiling water in an approximately 2:1 ratio. You will need about 1/2 to 1 cup of solution for each mason jar, depending on the size of the jar. Allow the solution to cool slightly, then pour the solution into the jars.
3. At this point, select a contaminant to add to one of your jars of sugar solution. Contaminants that you can add are food coloring or some corn syrup (about 1 tablespoon [tbsp] of either). Stir well.
4. Place the pencils and their strings or the skewers across the top of the mason jars (see Figure 2).
5. Place the jars in locations with stable conditions of temperature, sunlight, and air circulation such as on windowsills, inside dark cabinets, or on counter tops.

6. Check for crystals after 1 to 3 hours on day one, then check them once a day thereafter. Be sure not to disturb the jars.

7. After 5 to 7 days, remove the strings or skweres and allow them to dry.

8. Use a ruler to measure the largest crystal on each string or skewer. Record the measurements in your science notebook.

9. Count the number of crystals on each string or skewer and record the number in your science notebook.

10. Weigh two small pieces of paper towel and record the weights in your science notebook.

11. Using a plastic knife, gently scrape the crystals on one string or skewer onto one piece of paper towel. Repeat with the other string or skewer on the other paper towel.

12. Determine the weight of the crystals on one paper towel by subtracting the total weight from the weight of the paper towel alone. Repeat the procedure to find the weight of crystals on the other paper towel. Record the weights in your science notebook.

13. Examine some crystals from each string or skewer under the microscope. Describe what you see in your science notebook.

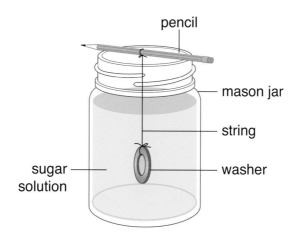

**Figure 2**

**A pencil supports the string in the Mason jar.**

## Analysis

1. Sketch a diagram of a single sugar crystal.

2. Describe the shape of the sugar crystals both each jar.

3. In which jar did the larger crystals grow? Why?

4.  In which jar did crystals form faster? Why?

5.  Which jar produced the most crystals by weight?

6.  Suggest a condition in which no crystal growth would occur.

## What's Going On?

Sugar is very soluble in water, but as the water evaporates from the syrupy solution, it will eventually reach a *saturation point*. It is at this concentration that sugar begins to *precipitate* from the solution. If the conditions are ideal, the precipitation event will not be random, which would result in an shapeless powder. Instead slow precipitation allows for single molecules to exchange from the solid to the dissolved phase repeatedly, until the molecule finds its place in the crystal lattice. Theoretically, it would be possible to grow a single crystal of sugar with a all the molecules in solution, given enough time for each individual sugar molecule to find its place in the lattice. What happens in reality is that multiple nucleation sites, solid surfaces around which crystals grow, form. As a result, crystals grow from each of these points. The rate of crystal growth depends on time as well as temperature, evaporation rate, and the presences of contaminants.

Table sugar is a *disaccharide*, a double sugar made of a glucose molecule linked to a fructose molecule (see Figure 3). Corn syrup is a very concentrated solution of a monosaccharide, glucose. Because corn syrup is close, but not quite the same, as the sugar syrup it will disrupt growth, preventing orderly packing.

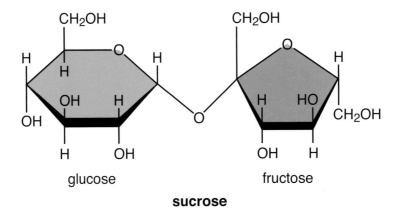

**Figure 3**

**Sucrose is made from a glucose molecule chemically bonded to a fructose molecule.**

## Connections

The business of growing crystals is clearly critical to candymakers. However, other professions grow crystals also. Crystal structures of compounds are invaluable to scientific research. In the process of *crystal diffraction*, scientists can peer into the heart of a well-ordered crystal and identify the precise locations of the atoms. Crystal structures also provide scientists with such important information as interatomic distances, the geometry of chemical bonds, and atomic composition. One common application of this information is the design of drugs to target specific *protein receptors*. The molecular shape of the receptor, once determined by X-ray crystallography, guides researchers in synthesizing small molecules that match the receptor. The pharmaceutical industry also employs crystallization to ensure the purity of the drugs we take. As was made clear from the addition of fructose in the experiment, contaminants interfere with the ability of a substance to crystallize. By crystallizing the drug molecule, any by-products and unreacted starting material that remains in solution can be filtered away.

Industry also employs crystallization and the analysis of crystal structure to deliver today's high-tech products. Analysis of the crystalline structure of metal in a car's engine block makes it possible to optimize the performance of the machine. Examination of the microstructure of steel can diagnose the early signs of stress and fatigue in critical pipelines and skyscraper skeletons. In the semiconductor industry, only the purest crystalline silicon is suitable for production of today's high-speed microprocessors. Without crystal structure analysis, the efficient machines and devices that are part of everyday life could not exist.

 ## Want to Know More?

See appendix for Our Findings.

## Further Reading

Barthelmy, David. Mineralogy Database, December 31, 2009. Available online. URL: http://webmineral.com/. Accessed September 25, 2010. This Web site lists thousands of minerals and provides pictures of their crystalline shapes.

Center for Computational Materials Science. "Crystal Lattice Structures," October 29, 2008. Available online. URL: http://cst-www.nrl.navy.mil/

lattice/. Accessed September 25, 2010. This Web site provides images of common crystal structures.

Freidman, Hershel. "Minerals A-Z," *The Mineral and Gemstome Kingdom* 2004. Available online. URL: http://www.minerals.net/mineral/index.htm. Accessed September 25, 2010. This detailed guide to minerals provides pictures and explanations on topics such as chemical groups, crystalline structures, and physical properties.

# 4. Erosion by Soil Type

## Topic

A given erosion-causing factor will affect some types of soil more than others.

## Introduction

Of the Earth's surface, only 37 percent is arable; that is, able to support plant growth. The arable area includes farmland as well as regions where forest, grasses, or shrubs grow. The two distinct features of such areas are soil type and water. Plants in arable land require both features. Ironically, water can be the primary culprit of *erosion,* the movement of *soil* and other solids by natural effects such as wind, ice, and water. Soil is a complex mixture of tiny rock pieces, minerals, organic matter from dead plants and animals, and living microbes.

Erosion is both a beneficial and a deleterious process. When mountains erode to form boulders, and boulders break down into rocks, and rocks are reduced to sand, erosion helps to build soil. However, soil erosion can threaten agricultural production. As the human population continues to expand, more lands are cleared to plant crops. Improperly managed farmlands are particularly vulnerable to soil erosion.

Soil conservationists want to understand conditions and situations that lead to water-based soil erosion and methods that can be employed to mitigate the problem. In this experiment, you will explore the effects of water erosion on various types of soil and other solid ground covers.

### Time Required

30 minutes

### Materials

- plastic rectangular box (such as disposable food storage container or shoebox)

- ice pick
- box cutter
- cookie sheet with edges
- 2 different dirt samples from students' yards, the school yard, a neighhood park, or other locations (about 3 cups of each)
- 4 door shims or wedges of wood
- soil of 2 types (about 6 cups [c] of each type)
- watering can with detachable sprinkler head
- water
- funnel coffee filters
- large plastic funnel
- ruler
- electronic balance
- science notebook

**Safety Note**  Take care when working with the ice pick and box cutter. Please review and follow the safety guidelines at the beginning of this volume.

## Procedure

1. Prepare the testing container. To do so:
   a. Use the box cutter to cut away one of the short ends of the plastic rectangular box, leaving about 1/4 inch (in.) (2/3 centimeters [cm]) at the sides and 1 in. (2.5 cm) at the bottom.
   b. Use the ice pick to punch holes in the bottom of the test container.
   c. Place test container on the cookie sheet
2. Place at least 1 in. of soil in the test container.
3. Fill the watering can with water.
4. Pour water from the watering can evenly onto soil.
5. Pour the water and soil that ran out of the test container onto the cookie sheet into the plastic funnel lined with a coffee filter.

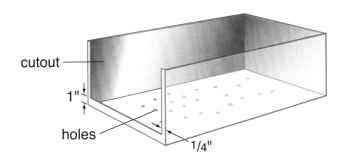

**Figure 1**

6.  After the water has drained from the soil, weigh the soil that has collected in the coffee filter. Record the weight in your science notebook.

7.  Use a ruler to measure the depth of any gullies created by erosion in the testing container. Record the results in your science notebook.

8.  Observe the test containers and experiment results of your classmates.

9.  Redistribute the soil in the container, then raise one end of the test container with door shims. Repeat steps 2 through 7.

10. Observe the test containers and experimental results of your classmates.

11. Pour out the soil in the testing container into a container designated by your teacher. Repeat steps 2 through 10 using a different kind of soil.

## Analysis

1.  Generally, which soil was most prone to erosion?

2.  How does slope affect the rate of erosion?

3.  Describe an experiment in which you compare the amount of erosion in sandy soil and in gravel.

4.  How do you think that ground cover such as moss or grass might affect rate and amount of erosion?

5.  What recommendations can you make for erosion control?

## What's Going On?

Erosion is a complex process with multiple causes. Flowing water is a primary causative agent of erosion. Water carries insoluble matter (such as soil and rocks) with it as it flows. The faster the water flow, or velocity, and the greater the water volume, the more erosion a given patch of land will experience. On the other hand, dry land becomes parched and cracked, as shown in Figure 2. Without water, a region cannot support plants, whose roots can slow or prevent erosion by holding together soil particles. As a result, soil turns to dust and is easily blown away.

Erosion can be reduced or prevented by several practices. Planting low-growing grasses and other small, soil-binding species of plants protects the soil. The root systems of plants also bind the soil together. Careful layering of nonliving matter can produce similar effects, particularly if the top layers are resistant to erosion but allow slow drainage to the soil beneath.

**Figure 2**

**Without plant roots to hold it together, the soil in a region can dry out and blow away.**

## Connections

Improper or unwise land use has always led to soil problems. One of the most dramatic examples is an event known as the *dust bowl*. During the 1930s, the overfarmed prairies of the American Midwest (see Figure 3) experienced prolonged droughts and massive wind storms. Unprotected *topsoil*, which took thousands of years to form, was blown into giant clouds of dust, reducing the fertility of the region. In recent years, Haiti has experienced similar problems. In Haiti, a growing population and uncontrolled clear cutting have resulted in deforestation of 98 percent of the nation's land. The steep slopes of unanchored soil can erode with alarming speed, often resulting in vast landslides and catastrophic destruction.

**Figures 3**

**During the 1930s drought and high winds caused the loss of topsoil in the Midwest.**

On the other hand, erosion can also sow the seeds of life as water and wind wear down rock and release minerals. Moving water can carry minerals down river and deposit them in fertile deltas. Such areas are prized for their agricultural potential. The "cradle of civilization," the area between the Tigris and the Euphrates rivers, presents exactly such a case where erosion has created a fecund land.

## Want to Know More?

See appendix for Our Findings.

## Further Reading

Huggins, David R., and John P. Reganold. "No-Till: How Farmers Are Saving the Soil by Parking Their Plows," 2010. Available online. URL: http://www.scientificamerican.com/article.cfm?id=no-till. Accessed September 25,

2010. In this July 2008 article, the authors point out how conventional farming increases soil erosion.

Pidwirny, Michael. *Fundamentals of Physical Geography,* 2nd ed., Chapter 10, "Introduction to the Lithosphere: Weathering," May 7, 2009. Available online. URL: http://www.physicalgeography.net/fundamentals/10r.html. Accessed September 25, 2010. Pidwirny discusses how weathering changes soil and explains the differences in physical and chemical weathering.

Soil Erosion Site, February 12, 2008. Available online. URL: http://soilerosion.net/. Accessed September 25, 2010. This Web site is a gateway that provides links to photographs, videos, and articles on soil erosion.

# 5. Mineral Identification

## Topic

The minerals that make up local rocks can be identified using several tests.

## Introduction

Some might refer to the ground we walk on as "just a bunch of rocks," but have you ever stopped to think about what materials make up those rocks? *Geologists*, scientists who study the materials that make up Earth, have given the question a lot of thought. Analysis shows that our Earth is composed of many different *minerals*, some of them quite valuable commercially. A mineral is a solid material that has a specific chemical composition and a defined crystal structure. Any *rock* is made of two or more minerals.

The Earth's surface is made up of more than 4,400 mineral types. People have known about many minerals since the dawn of civilization, and some of these minerals have even given their names to parts of our human history. For example, during the Stone Age our ancestors were experts at manipulating different rocks and minerals to create tools. Flint (microcrystalline quartz) was used to make arrowheads (see Figure 2) and to start fires, and tools were shaped from sharp pieces of obsidian (which is a mixture of $SiO_2$ with $MgO$ or $Fe_3O_4$).

**Figure 1**

**During the Stone Age, arrowheads were made of flint.**

After its formation, the young Earth had only about 250 different types of minerals, much fewer than are present today. Geologists know this from analysis of comets, meteors, and even some rocks that have remained unchanged from the time of Earth's formation 4.6 billion years ago. At that point, volcanic activity, which was driven by heat from impacts of meteors and from the radioactive decay of elements in the Earth itself, began producing new minerals. The constant melting and solidification of the Earth's *crust* purified some elements, yielding about 1,500 types of minerals, including many types of granite. These granitic minerals are lighter than the material of the Earth's *mantle,* so they float on the mantle and form the basis of the continents.

The next giant leap in mineral diversity occurred much later as tiny, single-celled organisms called *cyanobacteria*, began producing oxygen through the process of photosynthesis. As the concentration of atmospheric oxygen increased, most of the materials that make up Earth reacted with the oxygen and over 2,500 new types of minerals formed. As life evolved the types of minerals also changed. Coral reefs, coal, and limestone are all examples of minerals whose origin can be traced directly to biological activity.

In this experiment, you will find out what types of minerals are in your community by performing a series of tests on local rocks.

## Time Required

50 minutes

## Materials

- set of known minerals (for comparison)
- unknown rocks (several different rocks from the local area)
- U.S. coin
- pocketknife
- piece of glass
- hardened steel file
- sandpaper
- glazed tile

- 1 beaker (small)
- HCl (1 molar [M]) or vinegar (about 30 milliliters [ml])
- electronic balance
- graduated cylinder
- strong magnet
- hammer
- science notebook

**Safety Note** Wear goggles when working with acids. Take care when using the knife and working with the hammer. Please review and follow the safety guidelines at the beginning of this volume.

## Procedure

1. Select one unknown rock.
2. On the data table, record the color and luster (shine) of the unknown rock.
3. Figure 2 names the minerals used as standards for hardness on Mohs' Hardness Scale as well as the placement of some common items. Find the hardness of the unknown rock using the *Mohs' Hardness Scale* and record it on the data table in the column headed "hardness." To find the hardness:
   a. Try to scratch the mineral with your fingernail. If your nail scratches the rock, it has a hardness less than 2.5
   b. If your nail will not scratch the rock, try to scratch it with a coin. If a coin scratches the rock, it has a hardness of 2.6 to 3.0.
   c. If a coin will not scratch the rock, try to scratch it with a pocketknife. If a pocketknife scratches the rock, it has a hardness between 3.1 and 5.5.
   d. If a pocketknife will not scratch the rock, try to scratch it with a steel file. If successful, the rock's hardness is 5.6 to 6.5.
   e. If the pocketknife did not scratch the rock, try scratching it with sandpaper. If sandpaper leaves a scratch, the rock's hardness to 6.6 to 9.0. If not, the rock has a hardness greater than 9.0.
4. Test to see if the unknown test rock is magnetic. Hold the magnet near the test rock and observe any attraction. If the rock is attracted

to the magnet, write "yes" on the data table in the column titled "magnetic." If the rock is not attracted to the magnet, write "no" in the column.

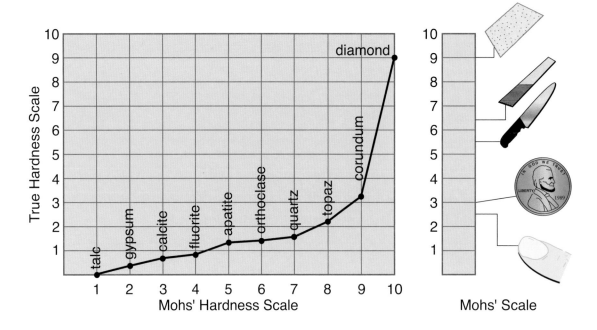

## Figure 2

### Mohs' Scale shows the hardness of minerals as well as some household items.

5. Test if the unknown rock is *carbonateous*, or contains carbon. Use the hammer to break off a few pieces of the rock. (A few milligrams [mg] will do.) Place the pieces into a small beaker containing dilute acid (1M HCl or vinegar). Watch for the production of bubbles for about 5 minutes (min). If bubbles are produced, write "yes" on the data table in the column headed "carbon." If bubbles are not produced, write "no."

6. Find the streak color for the unknown ock by dragging a flat face of the mineral across the glazed tile. In the last column of the data table, record the color of the mark left. If the mineral does not streak the tile, write "no streak."

7. Choose rocks from the known set of minerals with a similar color and luster as the unknown rock. Perform the tests in steps 3 through 6 on the known minerals until one is found with the same results.

8. Repeat steps 2 through 7 for two more unknown rocks.

| Data Table | | | | | | |
|---|---|---|---|---|---|---|
| | **Color** | **Luster** | **Hardness (Mohs' Scale)** | **Carbon** | **Magnetic** | **Streak color** |
| Rock 1 | | | | | | |
| Rock 2 | | | | | | |
| Rock 3 | | | | | | |

## Analysis

1. Based on your results, what are some of the minerals found in rocks in your area? Defend your determination.
2. Were any of the rocks magnetic? Which ones?
3. Were any of the rock carbonateous? Which ones?
4. What was the hardest rock?
5. What was the softest rock?

## What's Going On?

Minerals can be identified by several different means. The ones most easily accessible to you are luster (how it reflects light), color, and hardness (using the mohs' scale). In 1812, German mineralogist Friedrich Mohs (1773–1839) developed a scale to rate the hardness of minerals. The scale is relative, meaning you are comparing your sample to known test material. The Mohs' test tells you if the sample mineral you are testing is harder or softer than the test material. Crystal shape is also characteristic of minerals. For example, a quartz crystal, shown in Figure 3, is a six-sided hexagon.

In the carbonateous mineral test, the free protons of the acid react with carbonate ions ($CO_3^{2-}$) in the mineral to from water and $CO_2$, a gas that bubbles out of solution. This is a destructive test. Few minerals are magnetic; the most commonly encountered magnetic minerals are pure iron, iron-nickel, and magnetite (iron oxide, $Fe_3O_4$). Of these three, iron and iron-nickel do not occur naturally on Earth except in rare cases, but are found in meteorites. Some other ways to identify minerals include fracture pattern, streak color, magnetism, and density. Depending on the tools available to you, the more tests you can perform on an unknown mineral, the more confident you can be in any identification.

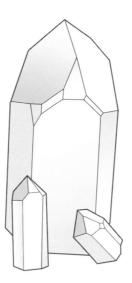

**Figure 3**

**Quartz crystals are six-sided hexagons.**

## Connections

Identification of minerals has long been a crucial skill for mankind. Being able to identify minerals, and more importantly know what properties of those minerals are useful, continues to be of great importance to our society today. Countries that are rich in mineral content become exporters of those riches. Heedless extraction of valuable minerals from the surrounding strata often has harmful environmental consequences. The task can also be dangerous to the workers.

The science of identifying rock formations and the minerals of value is associated with such formations is big business. One of the most lucrative examples of this is exploration for oil and natural gas deposits based on rock formations that are known to hold these resources. A solid knowledge base in geology is key to any serious mineral searching attempts.

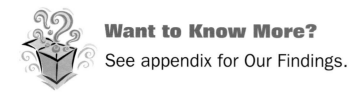

## Want to Know More?

See appendix for Our Findings.

## Further Reading

"Collector's Corner," 2010. Mineralogical Society of America. Available online. URL: http://www.minsocam.org/MSA/collectors_corner/ MineralCollecting.htm. Accessed September 25, 2010. This Web site explains how to begin a rock and mineral collection.

"Mineral Identification: Mohs Scale of Mineral Hardness." MineralTown. com. Available online. URL: http://www.mineraltown.com/infocoleccionar/ mohs_scale_of_hardness.htm. Accessed September 25, 2010. This Web site explains how to use Mohs' Scale to determine mineral hardness and provides the hardness of several different minerals.

Peck, Donald B. "The Rock Identification Key," 2001. Available online. URL: http://www.rockhounds.com/rockshop/rockkey/index.html. Accessed September 25, 2010. Peck explains the rock cycle and rock formation and gives descriptions of rock and mineral characteristics.

# 6. Soil Color and Temperature

## Topic

The color of soil affects the rate at which it absorbs and releases heat.

## Introduction

Many of the chemical and biological processes within an ecosystem occur inside the soil. The heat energy within soil has an impact on these processes. Soil absorbs heat from the radiant energy of the Sun. The amount of energy that soil takes up depends on numerous factors, including soil color, the amount and type of plant cover, and water content. The *angle of incidence*, which is the angle at which the Sun's rays hit the soil, also plays a role. The closer that angle is to 90 degrees (90°), the more energy the soil can absorb (see Figure 1). The amount of water in soil influences the rate at which soil warms or cools. Wet soil warms slower, and stays warm longer, than dry soil.

Soil temperature, a measure of its heat energy, is monitored by scientists for many reasons. Temperature influences the timing of seed *germination* in spring and leaf fall in autumn. Chemical reactions that occur in soil, such as decomposition, are influenced by temperature because, up to a point, the addition of heat speeds chemical processes. Temperature influences the emergence of insect larvae that feed on the roots, stems, and leaves of plants. In addition, *nitrification*, the process in which nitrogen gas is converted into nitrogen compounds that plants can use, does not occur until soil warms to about 40 degrees Fahrenheit (°F) (4.4 degrees Celsius [°C]), so cold temperatures limit this ecologically important process.

In this laboratory, you will design and perform an experiment to find out how one soil characteristic, color, affects soil temperature.

 **Time Required**

25 minutes on day 1
45 minutes on day 2

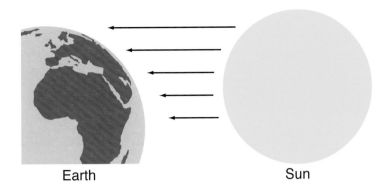

Earth                                    Sun

a. The Sun's energy does not strike all points on Earth at the same angle.

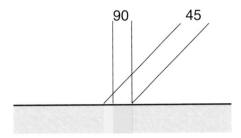

b. Near the equator, where the Sun's rays strike Earth with a 90° angle of incidence, the soil absorbs a lot of energy. Closer to the poles, the angle is more oblique, like the 45° angle shown here, and less energy strikes Earth.

**Figure 1**

## Materials

- ➡ sand (about 3 cups [c])
- ➡ large spoon
- ➡ 3 colors of food coloring
- ➡ 3 large beakers, bowls, or quart jars
- ➡ 3 soil thermometers
- ➡ gooseneck lamp with 75-watt bulb
- ➡ several sheets of newspaper
- ➡ tape
- ➡ ruler
- ➡ science notebook

**Safety Note** Please review and follow the safety guidelines at the beginning of this volume.

## Procedure

1. Your job is to design and perform an experiment to find out how the color of soil affects the rate at which soil absorbs heat. The soil provided for this experiment is sand. You can color some of the sand for your experimental procedure. To color sand:

   a. Fill a container, beaker, bowl, or jar about one-third full of sand.

   b. Add enough water to barely cover the sand.

   c. Add food coloring to the sand and water and stir to mix. Set the container aside to absorb the color. If desired, you can leave it overnight. The longer you let the container sit, the deeper the color will become.

   d. Pour off the excess water. Lay newspapers on a tabletop or floor, then spread the damp sand over the news paper. Leave the sand to dry overnight. The sand will be ready for use when the water evaporates.

2. You can use any of the supplies provided by your teacher, but you will not need to use all of them.

3. Before you conduct your experiment, decide exactly what you are going to do. Remember that you should have only one *variable* in your experiment, the color of the sand. Everything else must remain constant. Write the steps you plan to take (your experimental procedure) and the materials you plan to use (materials list) on Data Table 1. Show your procedure and materials list to the teacher.

4. If you get teacher approval on your experiment, answer Analysis questions 1 and 2. If not, modify your plan and show it to your teacher again.

5. Once you have teacher approval, answer analysis questions 1 and 2, then assemble the materials you need and begin your procedure.

6. Collect your results on a data table of your own design.

7. Answer Analysis questions 3 through 5.

| Data Table 1 | |
|---|---|
| **Your experimental procedure** | |
| **Your materials list** | |
| **Teacher's approval** | |

## Analysis

1. A *hypothesis* is a proposal or guess that explains an idea. What is your hypothesis in this experiment?

2. What variables must you control in this experiment?

3. Suzy suggested that instead of coloring sand, her group should go outdoors and dig up some dark soil and some light soil for this experiment. What is wrong with Suzy's idea?

4. Did your experimental results support your hypothesis? Explain your answer.

5. Describe a follow-up experiment to test one of the following hypotheses:

   a. Soil that is rich in organic matter absorbs more heat energy than soil that has a low organic content.

   b. Soil temperature and air temperature are the same at night.

   c. During the winter months, air temperature drops but soil temperature remains constant.

   d. Soil temperature is warmer than air temperature at *solar noon* when the Sun is highest in the sky.

## What's Going On?

In this experiment, you artificially colored the soil you used. However, in nature, soil color depends on the interactions of that soil with the *biotic* and *abiotic* elements of the ecosystem. Soil that is rich in organic matter is darker than soil without organic matter. Nitrogen-rich soil has a rich, dark color that is lacking in nitrogen-poor soil. If soil has been exposed to a lot of erosion, it loses much of its color so may be white, tan, or gray.

Your experiment demonstrated that dark soils absorb more energy than soil of light colors such as white, tan, yellow, or red. To understand why, you must think about light energy. The visible rays of sunlight are a mixture of colors. When sunlight strikes a dark object, most of the energy is absorbed and very little is reflected (see Figure 2). The absorbed energy raises the energy of the soil. This energy is converted and later emitted as a longer-wavelength form, *infrared energy*. The energy conversion process is explained by the *law of conservation of energy*, which says that energy cannot be created or lost, but it can change forms. Sunlight that strikes a light colored soil is primarily reflected, not absorbed.

## Connections

Color can provide information about the origin of soil and the chemical processes it has undergone. Soil color is due to complex interactions of

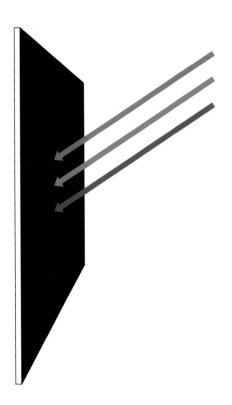

**Figure 2**

**Dark colored objects absorb all wavelengths of light.**

chemical and biological processes. The *surface horizon*s, or upper layers, of soils are primarily colored by biological processes like decomposition of organic matter. High levels of organic matter give soil a dark color.
On the other hand, subsoil color is primarily due to physical and chemical processes. Reactions involving water, iron, and other minerals create compounds that yield characteristics colors. Data Table 2 shows the correlation between color and the presence of organic matter or the action of chemical and physical activities.

Scientists evaluate the color of soil by examining three attributes, *hue*, *value*, and *chroma*, and comparing these attributes to a standardized scale called the *Munsell color system*. Hue is the result of a color's wavelength, value expresses how light or dark the soil is, and chroma describes the purity of the color. This system is used to express the *matrix,* or dominant soil type, in a sample. Some regions of the soil may be mottled, or spotted, with the primary color and other colors. The pattern of mottling may be due to drainage or aeration. Mottled regions can be found between productive surface soils and oxygen-poor, compacted soils. Figure 3 shows

| Data Table 2 | |
|---|---|
| **Soil Color** | **Cause** |
| Brown to black in the surface horizon | organic matter |
| Black in the subsoil | magnesium |
| Yellow to red in the subsoil | iron compounds in well-oxygenated, well-drained soil |
| Gray to blue-green in the subsoil | iron compounds in poorly oxygenated, poorly drained soil |
| White or gray in the subsoil | water soluble carbonate compounds |

how mottling separates the two soil regions and defines the area in which plant roots can survive. If mottling occurs nears the surface, the entire region probably suffers from poor drainage. Patterns of mottling found in deep soil suggest good drainage in the surface region.

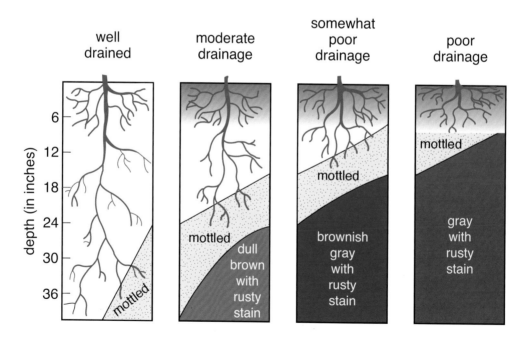

**Figure 3**

**Mottled soil can be found between productive soil that supports root growth and dull or gray soil that is oxygen poor.**

## Want to Know More?

See appendix for Our Findings.

## Further Reading

Fletcher, Peter C., and Peter L. M. Veneman. "Soil Morphology as an Indicator of Seasonal High Water Tables." Available online. URL: http://nesoil.com/properties/eshwt.htm. Accessed September 25, 2010. Fletcher and Veneman describe the characteristics of soil and explain the presence of colors.

Hons, Frank, Murray Milford, and Dave Zuberer. "Soil Basics 101," Organic Lifestyles. Available online. URL: http://organiclifestyles.tamu.edu/soilbasics/index.html. Accessed September 25, 2010. This Web site hosted by Texas A&M University provides information on soil's basic characteristics.

Lynn, W. C., and M. J. Pearson. "The Color of Soil." Natural Resources Conservation Service. Adapted from "The Color of Soil," *Science Teacher,* May 2000. Available online. URL: http://soils.usda.gov/education/resources/lessons/color/. Accessed September 25, 2010. The use of the Munsell color system is explained in this Web article.

# 7. Slope Stability

## Topic

The stability of a soil slope is affected by several factors including angle of the slope, type of soil particles, and the amount of water in the soil.

## Introduction

Hills are one of the most common *landforms* on Earth. Because hills are so widespread, they provide the foundations of millions of structures such as homes, businesses, and roads. The sides of hills form slopes. Those with low angles are stable and safe, but those with steep angles may suffer from erosion and slippage of soil that can lead to *landslides*. For this reason, the degree of hill slope may be measured before making plans for using the area.

Gravity is the major factor that determines a slope's stability. The force of gravity pulls everything toward the Earth's center. Regions of flat soil are pulled straight down by gravity and therefore do not move. Regions of soil sitting on a slope experience gravity as two components. As shown in Figure 1, one component ($G_p$) pulls straight down perpendicular to the slope and helps hold the soil in place. The other ($G_t$) is tangential to the slope in the direction of the slope and causes a *shear stress* on the soil. The steeper the slope, the greater the shear stress, and the less the stabilizing force of the gravitational pull.

As a group, all the forces that resist the slide of soil down a slope are known as the *shear strength*. These forces include *cohesion*, the attraction of soil particles to each other, and *friction*, the force that resists movement. If shear stress is greater than shear strength, a landslide can occur. Cohesion forces vary depending on soil type, location, and the amount of water on the slope.

In this laboratory, you will design an experiment to determine how one of these factors affects the likelihood that soil on a slope will slide.

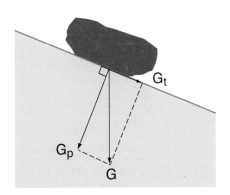

Figure 1

The stability of soil on a slope is influenced by both perpendicular ($G_p$) and tangential ($G_t$) gravitational forces.

## Time Required

35 minutes for part A
55 minutes for part B

## Materials

- sand (about 3 cups [c])
- clay soil (about 3 c)
- silty soil (about 3 c)
- loamy soil (about 3 c)
- cardboard (about 12 inches [in.]) [30.5 centimeters (cm) by 6 in. [15.2 cm]).
- prong paper file fastener
- protractor
- ruler
- scissors
- ice pick
- access to water

- newspapers

- large metal food can, clean, with both ends removed

- science notebook

## Procedure, Part A

1.  Create a pile of dry sand to use as a standard slope for comparison
    in this experiment. To do so:

    a. Spread newspapers on a tabletop or on the floor.

    b. Place the can in the center of the newspapers.

    c. Fill the can with dry sand.

    d. Gently lift the can. As you do, the sand in the can will create a
       pile with sloping sides.

2.  Make an angle-measuring tool. To do so:

    a. Cut out two strips of cardboard, each about 6 in. (15.2 cm) long
       by 1 in. (2.5 cm) wide.

    b. Carefully, use the ice pick to punch a hole in one end of each
       strip of cardboard. The hole should be about 0.5 in. (1.2 cm)
       from one end.

    c. Attach the two pieces of cardboard with the paper file fastener so
       that they can rotate around the fastener (see Figure 2).

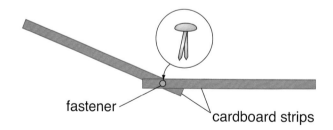

fastener        cardboard strips

**Figure 2**

**An angle-measuring device can be used to compare
the steepness of slopes.**

3.   Measure the angle of the slope. To do so, position the angle-measuring tool next to the sand pile, as shown in Figure 3, with one piece of cardboard on the floor or table top next to the pile of sand and the other piece extended along the edge of the pile of sand.

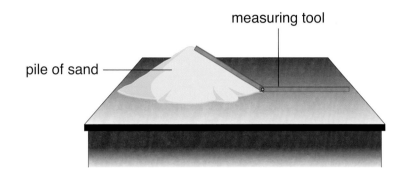

measuring tool

pile of sand

**Figure 3**

**Position the angle-measuring device so that one arm is on the floor or desktop and the other arm lies along the slope of the pile of soil.**

4.   Remove the tool, holding the pieces of cardboard in position. Compare the position of the angle created by the tool to a protractor. Record the angle as angle $A$ in your science notebook. Answer Analysis question 1.

## Procedure, Part B

1.   Your job is to design and perform an experiment to find out how one variable affects angle $A$ on a pile of sand. You will use the angle created by the sand in part A of the procedure as a control. Variables could include, but are not limited to, the addition of water (in the amount you select) to the soil or variation in soil composition. Working with your lab group, decide on the variable you will test. For example, you might want to find if the addition of dry clay particles to the sand affects slope stability. Once you have an idea of what you want to test in your experiment, answer Analysis question 2.

2.   You can use any of the supplies provided by your teacher, but you may not need to use all of them.

3.   Before you conduct your experiment, decide exactly what you are going to do. Write the steps you plan to take (your experimental procedure) and the materials you plan to use (materials list) on the

data table. Show your procedure and materials list to the teacher. If you get teacher approval, proceed with your experiment. If not, modify your work and show it to your teacher again.

4.  Once you have teacher approval, assemble the materials you need and begin your procedure.

5.  Collect your results on a data table of your own design.

6.  Answer Analysis questions 3 through 6.

| Data Table | |
|---|---|
| **Your experimental procedure** | |
| **Your materials list** | |
| **Teacher's approval** | |

## Analysis

1.  In part A of the procedure, how many degrees is angle *A*?

2.  What is the hypothesis of your experiment?

3.  Why is it important to test only one variable at a time?

4. Was the angle produced by your experiment in part B of the procedure larger or smaller than angle *A* in part A?

5. Did your conclusion support your hypothesis? Why or why not.

6. Describe a follow-up experiment for the one you just performed.

## What's Going On?

If you have ever built a sand castle at the beach or in a backyard sandbox, you probably used damp sand. With moist sand, you could build a castle with straight sides and turrets around the top. Such an engineering feat would be impossible if the sand were dry. The explanation for this phenomenon is related to the *cohesion* of water molecules and to friction.

Soil particles are ordinarily interspersed with lightweight pockets of air. Water adds weight to the soil because it seeps between the sand particles and replaces the air trapped there. Weight is a force that is influenced by the pulled of gravity, so the addition of water, up to a point, helps stabilize a slope. Also, the *surface tension* of water molecules helps hold the grains together. Water is a *polar* compound, so water molecules are attracted to each other. When sand particles are covered in a film of water, the attraction of water molecules holds the particles in place.

When a pile of sand is dry, the stability is largely due to the frictional forces between individual grains. This frictional force increases as grain size increases, so a pile of dry sand can have a steeper slope than a pile of dry silt.

## Connections

Landslides can result from natural causes, such as the geology of the region and severe rainfall. However, humans are to blame for many landslides. Modifications in the shapes of slopes and the removal of trees and other plants can lead to landslides. Vegetation increases slope strength by holding together soil particles. In February 2006, more than 1,000 people died when they were buried in mud from a landslide on Leyte Island, Philippines. Blame for the event was laid on the removal of trees from the region without replanting. Trees and other plants send roots into the soil that help hold it in place. In addition, excess water in the soil is taken up by roots and released by evaporation through tree leaves, helping stabilize the region. In October of 2010, torrential rains from typhoon Fanapi caused landslides and flooding in eastern China. On the island of Taiwan, residents fled to the mountains to escape the flooded lowlands. However, mountainous regions offered little safety because they are prone to landslides during periods of heavy rain. As a result, 18 people died and at least 44 were seriously injured by the storm.

Disturbances such as earthquakes and volcanoes can cause landslides by shaking the soil and underlying rock so severely that unconsolidated material may displaced. In May 2008, Beichuan, China, experienced a severe quake that registered 7.9 on the Richter scale. Aftershocks of the events caused devastating landslides that buried cities and killed hundreds of residents.

## Want to Know More?

See appendix for Our Findings.

## Further Reading

Conde, Carlos H. "Danger of Philippine Landslides Often Ignored, Critics Say," February 21 2006. *New York Times*. Available online. URL: http://www.nytimes.com/2006/02/21/international/asia/21filip.html?_r=1. Accessed September 25, 2010. In the Philippines, deforestation for commercial harvesting of trees has left the countryside denuded, increasing the danger of landslides, as this article explains.

Horton, Jennifer. "How Landslides Work," 2010. HowStuffWorks. Available online. URLhttp://science.howstuffworks.com/environmental/earth/geology/landslide.htm. Accessed September 25, 2010. An animation of a landslide can be found on this Web page.

USGS. "Landslide Events," April 15, 2010. Available online. URL: http://landslides.usgs.gov/recent/. Accessed September 25, 2010. This Web site has links to news coverage of landslides from 2004 to the present.

# 8. Erosion on Sand Dunes

## Topic

Wind erosion on sand dunes can be reduced with fencing.

## Introduction

Wind can transport unconsolidated fragments of soil. Small soil particles, like *silt,* can be picked up and carried long distances. However sand particles are relatively heavy compared to other types of soil, so they are not carried as far. As a result, windblown sand travels only a short distance before being dropped. In a short time, the sand particles are picked up again, then dropped. This hopping form of transport, shown in Figure 1, is characteristic of sand and is called *saltation*.

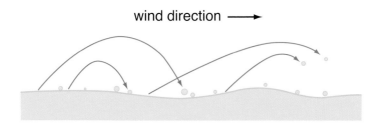

**Figure 1**

**Wind picks up sand particles and moves them a short distance.**

Mounds of sand that are piled up by wind form *sand dune*s. Most often, dunes develop in areas where sand is dry. Dunes are not symmetrical structures. They are flattened on the windward-facing back side. As the wind moves up the slope, it travels and over the top to the steeply sloping front side (see Figure 2). As wind moves down the front of the dune, it slows and drops the sand particles it is carrying. Over time, sand is continuously picked up on the back side and carried to the front, causing the dune to be eroded on the upwind side and grow on the downwind side. As a consequence, dunes travel downwind. In this experiment, you will find out how sand particles are affected by wind and compare the effectiveness of two barriers that are commonly used to slow sand erosion.

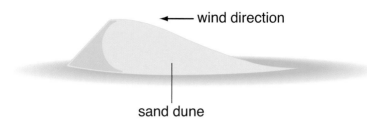

**Figure 2**

**Sand blows up the slope and is deposited on the steep front of the dune.**

## Time Required

65 minutes

## Materials

- ⮑ large, shallow plastic box (such as a storage container) without a lid, at least 3 feet (ft) (1 meter [m]) long and about 6 inches [in.] (15 centimeters [cm]) deep
- ⮑ sand (enough to fill the plastic box to a depth of about 4 in. [10 cm])
- ⮑ Popsicle™ sticks (about 1 dozen)
- ⮑ string (about 3 ft) (1 meter [m])
- ⮑ fabric (a few thin strips)
- ⮑ ruler
- ⮑ battery-powered fan
- ⮑ extension cord
- ⮑ clock with a second hand or timer
- ⮑ access to an outdoor area
- ⮑ science notebook

**Safety Note**    Be careful when working with the fan. Stay with your teacher in the outdoor area. Please review and follow the safety guidelines at the beginning of this volume.

## Procedure

1. Follow your teachers to an outdoor area where you will be carrying out this experiment. Working with a group, place sand in the plastic box to a depth of about 4 in. (10 cm). Spread the sand so that the top is smooth.

2. In your science notebook, draw the appearance of the sand in the box. Take measurements of the sand depth at several locations and record the depths in your science notebook.

3. Position the fan at one end of the box. Turn on the fan for 3 minutes (min) and observe what happens to the sand.

4. After 3 min, turn off the fan. Some of the sand has most likely changed position. Draw the appearance of the sand. Take measurements of the sand depth at several locations and record these depths on the drawing. As you are taking your measurements, do not change the position of the sand in any way. Note the area(s) where the most sand was lost.

5. Repeat steps 3 and 4 for another 3 min for a total of 6 min.

6. Repeat steps 3 and 4 for another 3 min for a total of 9 min.

7. Answer Analysis questions 1 through 3.

8. Smooth the sand so that it looks like it did in step 2. If necessary, add more sand.

9. Place a row of Popsicle™ sticks across the area of sand where there was substantial loss due to wind erosion.

10. Repeat steps 3 through 6.

11. Answer Analysis question 4.

12. Remove the Popsicle™ sticks and attach a strip of fabric to them using glue or staples.

13. Smooth the sand so that it looks like it did in step 2. If necessary, add more sand. Return the Popsicle™ sticks to the same locations as in step 9.

14. Repeat steps 3 through 6.

15. Answer Analysis questions 5 through 7.

## Analysis

1. How did the arrangement of the sand in the box change after 3 min?

2. How did the arrangement of the sand in the box change after 6 min?

3.  How did the arrangement of the sand in the box change after 9 min?

4.  How did the Popsicle™ sticks affect the amount of sand that was moved after 3, 6, and 9 min of exposure to wind from the fan?

5.  How did the fabric attached to the Popsicle™ sticks affect the amount of sand that was moved after 3, 6, and 9 min of exposure to wind from the fan?

6.  If you were in charge of reducing erosion of sand dunes at the beach, what would you do? Be specific in your plan.

7.  On some beaches, it is illegal to remove plants like sea oats from the dunes. Why do you think this is so?

## What's Going On?

The fan simulates a wind blowing across an area of dry, unconsolidated sand. Strong wind is capable of picking up sand particles and carrying them a short distance. In this experiment, the unprotected sand was blown by the wind and moved toward the far end of the plastic box. The addition of Popsicle™ sticks to the sand acted as speed bumps and reduced the wind's velocity. Addition of fabric to the sticks further interrupted the wind's strength.

In natural environments, ripples may appear as small sand particles are transported away and larger ones are left. Ripples form perpendicular to the direction in which the wind is blowing. The sand being carried by wind is deposited when the wind speed slows. Natural irregularities in sandy regions slow the wind's speed, causing deposition. Objects in the sand such as small plants or rocks can also cause deposition, which can form a mound.

## Connections

Sand is deposited on beaches by onshore currents. During low tide, when the sand dries, wind picks up a few grains at a time, carrying it closer to shore to form sand dunes. The process of dune formation is slow and can take decades. Newly formed, shallow dunes are known as *embryo dunes*. Embryo dunes begin as sand accumulates around protruding materials on the beach like rocks, piles of seaweed, or dead birds. Over time, if the young dunes persist, drought-resistant grasses take root.

The presence of grasses can stabilize young dunes so much that they grow to heights of 15 ft (5 m) or more. Once established, dunes are able to support other *pioneer plants* such as saltwort. The root systems of grasses and saltwort plants are extensive and capable of holding together sand particles. As plants and animals die, their bodies are broken down by bacteria, fungi, and a variety of scavengers, changing the make-up of the soil. The organic matter enriches the soil, making it possible for other plants to become established. Over time, insects move in, providing food for birds and small lizards.

Even though sand dunes have value as geological formations and as unique ecosystems, they are under threat from human activity. The locations of dunes between the ocean and inland areas mean that they experience a lot of human traffic. The more dunes are disturbed, the easier it is for them to be damaged. In some regions, dune fences have been installed to prevent sand loss (see Figure 3). Fences slow the velocity of sand-carrying wind, causing the sand particles to drop out. Fences are most effective if they are erected in line with the natural vegetation. Straight fences that run parallel to the shore are better at blocking wind than those with zigzag arrangements. A fence that is 4 ft (1.2 m) tall will generally be filled in with sand within a period of two years.

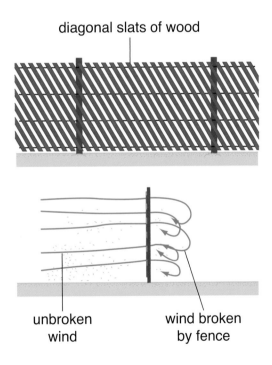

**Figure 3**

**Slats of wood in fencing slow down wind and cause the deposition of sand.**

## Want to Know More?

See appendix for Our Findings.

## Further Reading

Armstrong, Wayne P. "The Life and Love of Sand Dunes," 2010. Available online. URL: http://www.desertusa.com/magjan98/dunes/jan_dune1. html. Accessed September 25, 2010. Armstrong, a professor at Palomar College, San Marcos, California, discusses several types of desert sand dunes.

Pidwirny, Michael. "Eolian processes and landforms," February 2, 2007. Available online. URL: http://www.eoearth.org/article/Eolian_processes_ and_landforms. Accessed September 25, 2010. Pidwirny explains the mechanics behind erosion and deposition by wind.

Ronca, Debra. "How Sand Dunes Work," 2010. HowStuffWorks. Available online. URL: http://geography.howstuffworks.com/terms-and-associations/sand-dune.htm/printable. Accessed September 25, 2010. This Web site describes several types of sand dunes and provides video that explains their formation.

# 9. Naming Rocks

## Topic

Rocks can be identified using a rock key.

## Introduction

A rock is a naturally occurring aggregate of two or more minerals. If you find a rock outside the school, how can you identify it? The first thing to do is to determine in which of the three large groups the rock fits: *igneous*, *metamorphic*, or *sedimentary*. Igneous rocks were formed when hot, melted rock cooled and solidified. These rocks are hard and usually dark in color. Igneous rocks may have visible grains, look like black glass, or have a bubbly texture. Granite, obsidian, and basalt are examples of igneous rocks.

Metamorphic rocks were created when existing rock was subjected to heat and pressure, causing them to change. The resulting rocks have a variety of colors. Some, like slate, show *foliation*, or layering. Others, including marble, are hard and have a pearly luster. The term *luster* is used to describe the way a rock or mineral interacts with light. Rocks exhibit a variety of lusters, including metallic luster, which means that the rock shines like a piece of metal, or earthy luster, describing a mineral looks like dried mud.

Sedimentary rocks were made either of particles of preexisting rock that were deposited then compacted or from minerals that *precipitated* from a body of water. The colors of sedimentary rocks vary from light shades to gray or brown. Some sedimentary rocks contain *carbonates*, minerals that contain the $CO_3^{2-}$ ion. If acid is dripped on these rocks, bubbling occurs as the carbonates react with the acid.

In the field, a rock may be identified using a rock key. An identification key uses a series of yes-no questions. In this experiment, you will use a rock identification key to determine the names of several rocks. Then you will develop your own identification key.

## Time Required

55 minutes

## Materials

- ⚬ large beaker or bowl (cereal size)
- ⚬ access to water
- ⚬ dropper bottle of vinegar or 10 percent hydrochloric acid
- ⚬ hand lens
- ⚬ 3 groups of rock samples:
  - ✔ igneous rocks
  - ✔ metamorphic rocks
  - ✔ sedimentary rocks (which have been labeled with their names)
- ⚬ small hammer
- ⚬ gloves
- ⚬ goggles
- ⚬ science notebook

**Safety Note**    Take care when working with acid; wear gloves and goggles. Please review and follow the safety guidelines at the beginning of this volume.

## Procedure

1. Determine the name of each igneous rock using the Igneous Rock Key. Each step of the key posits two statements about a rock. When you select the correct statement, you will be given directions to go to another question, or you will be given the name of the rock. If necessary, use the hand lens to help you examine the rock samples.

2. Answer Analysis questions 1 and 2.

| **Igneous Rock Key** | |
|---|---|
| 1. a. Individual rock crystals are visible.<br>   b. Individual rock crystals are not visible. | go to 2<br>go to 3 |
| 2. a. Crystals are large.<br>   b. Crystals are small. | granite<br>rhyolite |
| 3. a. Rock does not have a shiny or glassy appearance.<br>   b. Rock is shiny or glassy. | go to 4<br>obsidian |
| 4. a. Rock is heavy and will not float.<br>   b. Rock is light and floats. | basalt<br>go to 5 |
| 5. a. Rock is a light color with small bubbles.<br>   b. Rock is a dark color with large bubbles. | pumice<br>scoria |

3. Determine the names of the individual metamorphic rocks using the Metamorphic Rock Key. If necessary, use the hand lens to help you examine the rock samples.

4. Answer Analysis questions 3 and 4.

| **Metamorphic Rock Key** | |
|---|---|
| 1. a. Rock has foliations (layers).<br>   b. Rock lack foliations. | go to 2<br>go to 3 |
| 2. a. Rock has a dull luster.<br>   b. Rock lacks a luster and has visible grains. | slate<br>go to 4 |
| 3. a. Using a magnifying glass, rock is grainy.<br>   b. Rock has crystals and a pearly luster. | quartzite<br>marble |
| 4. a. Rock has alternating light and dark bands.<br>   b. Rock flakes into layers. | gneiss<br>schist |

5.  Examine the sedimentary rocks, which have been labeled with their names. Develop a key of your own for this group of rocks. Characteristics that you might want to use in your sedimentary rock key include the presence or absence of layers, the size of individual particles in the rocks, and whether or not a little acid dropped onto the rock produces bubbles.

6.  Answer Analysis questions 5 and 6.

## Analysis

1.  Pumice and obsidian are both made from magma that cooled. Describe the difference(s) in their appearance. What might have caused this difference(s)?

2.  Why do you think that pumice and scoria float?

3.  One of the metamorphic rocks produces a "tink" sound when gently struck or thumped. Which rock is it?

4.  Compare the schist to gneiss. What is one clear difference in these rocks?

5.  In which sedimentary rocks can you see layers?

6.  In which sedimentary rocks are individual particles visible?

7.  Which sedimentary rocks produce bubbles when exposed to acid?

## What's Going On?

A rock key is a valuable field instrument that can help you identify rocks by their appearance or chemical properties. The characteristics of igneous rock are due to the rate of cooling and pressure during their formative period. Glassy rock such as obsidian and bubbly rock like pumice cooled quickly on the surface. Rock that cooled more slowly had time to develop crystals. Basalt and rhyolite are two igneous rocks that formed slowly near the surface. These rocks have relatively fine grains. Granite is an igneous rock that has coarser grains because it formed deeper in the Earth where it cooled very slowly, giving the grains time to grow.

Metamorphic rock is created when existing rock is put under extreme heat or pressure. The amount of heat and pressure affect the final product (see Figure 1). Slate is a metamorphic rock with foliation and a dull luster. Marble, schist, and quartzite, which were exposed to more heat and pressure than slate, lack visible foliation. Gneiss, which formed under extreme heat and pressure, is the hardest sedimentary rock in this experiment.

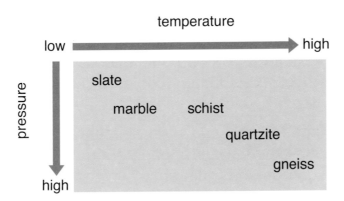

**Figure 1**

**Metamorphic rocks**

When sand, silt, or clay particles are worn away, redeposited, and put under pressure, they form sedimentary rock. The size of the rock grains determines the type of rock (see Figure 2). Shale and mudstone are formed from very small particles. The particles that make up sandstone and conglomerate are larger. Limestone and dolomite are both carbonates. Although there is some disagreement among geologists as to how dolomite formed, all agree that limestone results from the deposition of skeletal remains of sea organisms. Both minerals react with acids to produce bubbles, but dolomite does so very slowly.

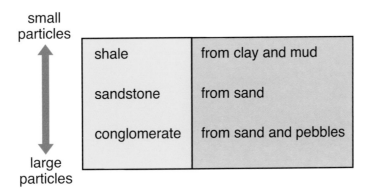

**Figure 2**

**Sedimentary rocks**

## Connections

The condition of rocks on Earth's surface is not static. Rocks are changed through a sequence of events called the *rock cycle*, an ongoing process that has no beginning or end. Some parts of the rock cycle occur very slowly over millions of years, but in some instances we can see the rock cycle in action. For example, the eruption of an Icelandic volcano in 2010 sent hot lava, ash, and gases into the atmosphere. Most of the magma associated with this geologic hot spot never makes it to the surface, but cools slowly underground to form a rock called *gabbro*. However, the lava that runs down the volcano's slopes cools quickly, creating a new layer of basalt.

The basalt on the surface is exposed to the elements, which begin breaking it down into fine grains. Over a long period of time, these small particles will be carried some distance by wind or water and redeposited. For the gabbro to erode, it must first be uplifted and all of the material covering it worn away; this process takes longer. In both cases, the resulting particles are deposited, forming sedimentary layers that become heavier and heavier, compressing the deepest layers into rocks. Sedimentary rocks may be uplifted, after which they are exposed to erosion again.

Rocks along the edges of some *tectonic plates* are *subducted*, or pushed underneath other plates where pressure melts them. This melted rock can be pushed upward as new metamorphic rock or can erupt through volcanic processes to form new igneous rock. In this way, the process begins again (see Figure 3).

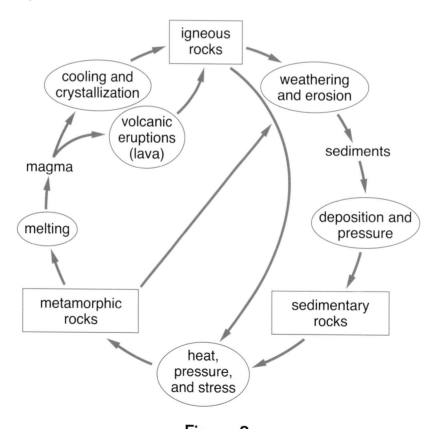

**Figure 3**

**The rock cycle**

## Want to Know More?

See appendix for Our Findings.

## Further Reading

Glendale Community College. "Earth Science Image Archive." Available online. URL: http://gccweb.gccaz.edu/earthsci/imagearchive/igneous.htm. Accessed September 25, 2010. Descriptions and photographs of rocks are provided on this Web site.

Gore, Pamela J. W. "Sedimentary Rocks," 2008. Available online. URL: http://facstaff.gpc.edu/~pgore/geology/geo101/sedrx.htm. Accessed September 25, 2010. Gore, of Georgia Perimeter College, describes the different groups of sedimentary rocks and provides excellent photographs.

Berndl, Elfi, and Nicholas Gere. "Identifying Minerals," 2010. RocksForKids. Available online. URL: http://www.rocksforkids.com/RFK/identification.html. Accessed September 25, 2010. This Web site provides definitions, pictures, and links to information about different types of rocks.

# 10. Rock Deformation

## Topic

Rock layers in the Earth's crust are rearranged by heat and pressure.

## Introduction

The Earth's *crust*, its outermost layer, is constantly changing. Rocks in the crust are pushed and pulled by stressors such as high temperatures and intense pressure. As a result of the stressors, layers of rock in the crust are altered, sometimes creating *faults* (breaks) and *folds* (buckles). Geologists, scientists who study rocks, divide stress on rocks into four types (see Figure 1).

1.  Isostatic stress is equal in all directions. This type of stress causes changes in rock volume but not in shape.

2.  Compressive stress squeezes rock and causes folds or faults. Regions of the crust that are exposed to compressive stress are thickened.

3.  Tensile stress pulls the crust in opposite directions, causing elongation. Regions of the crust exposed to tensile stress are thinned. Extensive tensile stress can cause faults.

4.  Shear stress pushes or pulls the crust in two opposite directions. For example, shear stress might distort a cube of rock into a rhomboid shape.

The folds produced by stress may be symmetrical, asymmetrical, overturned, or recumbent, as shown in Figure 2. Each fold shows certain elements of anatomy. The *axial plane* is the imaginary line that divides the fold into two halves, and the fold axis or hinge is the area of greatest curvature. The limbs are the sides of the fold. Folds in rock layers that are concave upward are called *synclines*. Those with strata that are concave downward are called *anticlines* (see Figure 3). In this experiment, you will find out how compressive forces create folds in the Earth's crust.

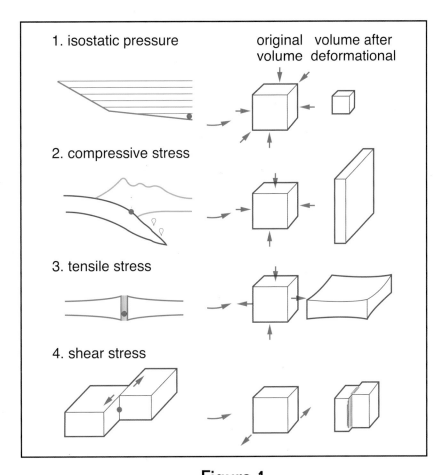

## Figure 1

## Pressure and stress affect the volume and shape of sections of the crust.

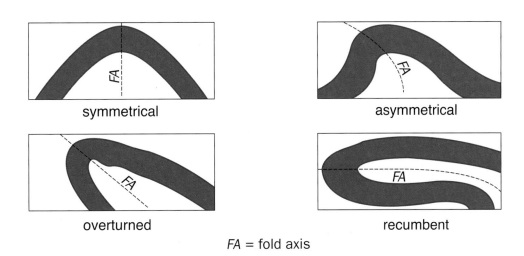

FA = fold axis

## Figure 2

## Types of folds found in rock layers

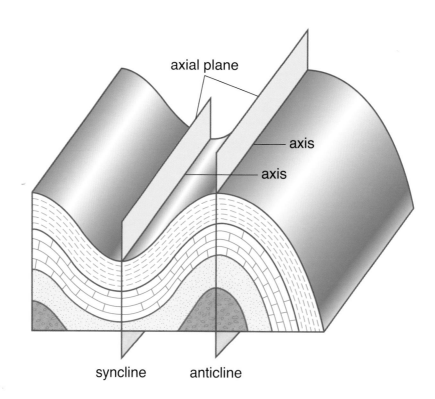

## Figure 3

**Folds that are concave upward are synclines. Folds that are concave downward are anticlines.**

## Time Required

30 minutes for part A
45 minutes for part B

## Materials

- red Play-Doh™ or clay (about 1/2 cup [c])
- blue Play-Doh™ or clay (about 1/2 c)
- green Play-Doh™ or clay (about 1/2 c)
- yellow Play-Doh™ or clay (about 1/2 c)
- plastic knife
- waxed paper
- colored pencils

- rolling pin
- scissors
- tape
- glue
- photocopy of Figure 5
- science notebook

**Safety Note** Please review and follow the safety guidelines at the beginning of this volume.

## Procedure, Part A

1.  Spread a layer of waxed paper on your desktop.

2.  Use the rolling pin to roll each color of Play-Doh™ or clay into a layer that is about 0.5 inches (in.) (1 centimeter [cm]) thick. Make all four layers about the same size and shape.

3.  Stack the layers in this order, red (bottom-most layer), blue, green, and yellow, to form one stratified block of clay.

4.  Exert compressional force on the block of Play-Doh™ or clay. To do so, place your hands on two sides. Slowly push toward the center, observing any changes that occur in block. Stop pushing once a fold develops.

5.  To show how a fold might look from the top after years of *erosion*, very carefully slice off about 0.5 in. (1 cm) of Play-Doh™ or clay from the top. (*Hint*: You may have to turn the block on its side to slice it.)

6.  Look down on the top of the block and compare it to the front, then draw the top and the front in your science notebook, using colored pencils.

7.  To show further erosion to the block, very carefully slice off about 1 in. (2.5 cm) of Play-Doh™ or clay.

8.  Look down on the top of the block and compare it to the front, then draw what you see in your science notebook, using colored pencils.

9.  Repeat steps 7 and 8.

10. When you have finished your drawings, separate the colors of Play-Doh™ or clay and roll each color into a 0.5 in. (1 cm) layer.

**11.** Use the clay to demonstrate how an adjacent syncline and anticline might be formed.

## Procedure, Part B

**1.** Cut out the boxes from a photocopy of Figure 5 along the solid lines. Each box represents a block of the crust that includes a fold structure.

**2.** Box A shows the structures on the front of a block. Based on the structures provided, draw the structures on the other four sides.

**3.** Color the sides and the top of each box using appropriate colors.

**4.** Fold on the dotted line and tape or glue together the box.

**5.** Box B shows the structure on the top of a block. Draw the structures on the other four sides of this block.

**6.** Repeat steps 3 and 4.

## Analysis

**1.** Figure 4 shows blocks of rock in Earth's crust. Examine the folds in each block and label them as either synclines or anticlines. Then label each as symmetrical, asymmetrical, overturned, or recumbent.

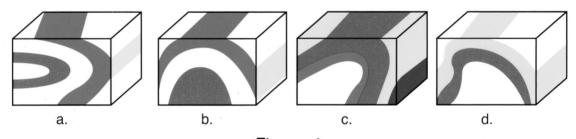

a.                    b.                    c.                    d.

**Figure 4**

**2.** What type of fold did the compressive forces of your hands produce on the clay: symmetrical, asymmetrical, overturned, or recumbent?

**3.** Explain how you demonstrated the formation of an adjacent anticline and syncline in step 11.

**4.** Geologists can view rock layers from the top and visualize how the rock is folded underground. You modeled this type of visualization by recreating the three-dimensional aspects of folds when you colored the structures in Figure 5. What type of fold is found in structure A? in structure B?

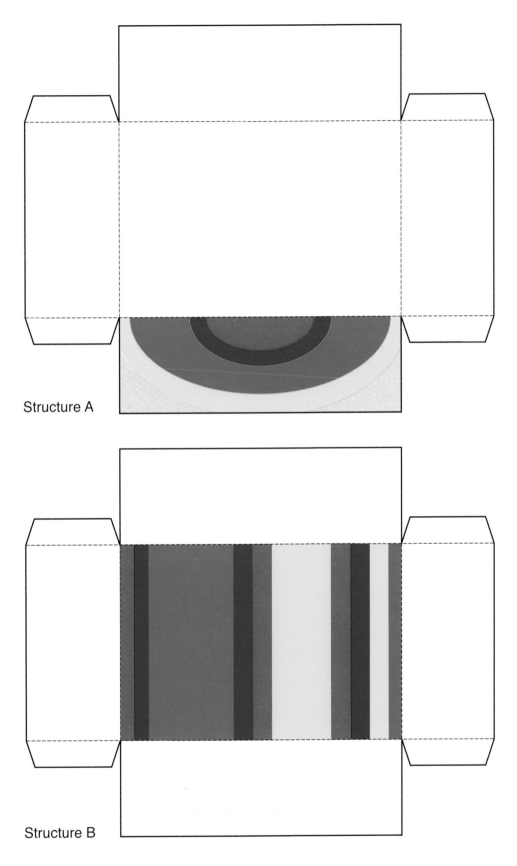

Structure A

Structure B

**Figure 5**

## What's Going On?

In this experiment, you demonstrated how folds can be produced in the Earth's crust. The four layers of clay represented four layers of rock in the crust. When you compressed the clay, you created one or more folds.

Geologists' viewing geological structures from the surface are rarely able to see the entire, three-dimensional structure. As a result, they use their knowledge of folding to predict the appearance of rock layers underground. You predicted the three-dimensional shapes of rock layers by creating fold structures made from folded paper. In structure A, you could see an anticline on the front of the block. Structure B, which is more complex, shows the top of a syncline adjacent to an anticline.

## Connections

Geologists need to understand the arrangement of rock layers beneath the surface for practical reasons. By locating folds in the crust, geologists can also find fossils fuels, groundwater, and deposits of minerals. Accuracy in identifying fold structures can prevent drilling in the wrong places and save hundreds of thousands of dollars.

Geologists searching for oil and natural gas know that these fossil fuels have a low density and tend to move upward through the Earth's crust. Unless the materials are trapped by impermeable rock layers, they will eventually reach the surface. Some folds are ideal at trapping these fuels. Anticlines, which are made up of permeable, oil-containing layers that are wedged between impermeable rock layers, will hold oil in the hinge region of the fold. Natural gas, which is less dense than oil, will rise to the top of the hinge (see Figure 6). Geologists can locate anticlines by examination of rocks of the surface.

 **Want to Know More?**

See appendix for Our Findings.

## Further Reading

Delta Mine Training Center. "Oil Deposit Characterization." Available online. URL: http://www.dmtcalaska.org/exploration/ISU/unit5/

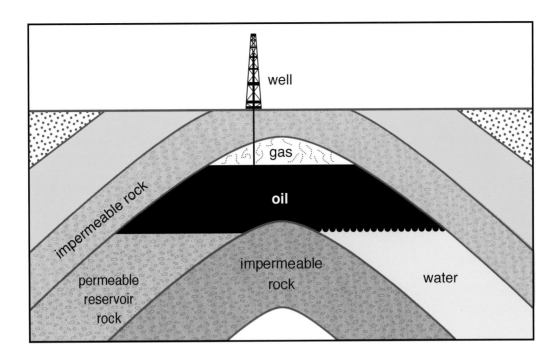

**Figure 6**

**Oil and natural gas can be trapped in the hinge area of a syncline.**

u5lesson1.html. Accessed September 25, 2010. This advanced lesson for students in the mineral industry explains how oil is formed and trapped in folds of rock.

Mantei, Erwin J. "Geologic Structures." Available online. URL: http://courses.missouristate.edu/EMantei/creative/glg110/GeoStruct.html. Accessed September 25, 2010. On this Web site, by Dr. Mantei of Missouri State University, discusses several geologic structures, including synclines and anticlines, and provides photographs.

Pidwirny, Michael. "Crustal Deformation Processes: Folding and Faulting," *Fundamentals of Physical Geology*, 2nd ed. PhysicalGeography. Net., 2006. Available online. URL: http://www.physicalgeography.net/fundamentals/10l.html. Accessed September 25, 2010. Dr. Pidwirny explains how rock layers form folds and faults and provides a photograph of a synclinal fold.

# 11. Half-life in Rock Dating

## Topic

The age of rocks can be determined through the analysis of radioactive components.

## Introduction

Dinosaurs lived about 230 million years ago. Scientists know this from their studies of fossils buried deep within layers of rock. Through the process *radiometric dating*, scientists can determine the ages of rocks and fossils. This technique compares the abundance of naturally occurring radioactive materials to the abundance of their breakdown products. Radiometric dating is possible because both rocks and fossils are made of atoms, the smallest particles of an element. Atoms are made up of three types of subatomic particles: protons and neutrons in the central nucleus and electrons in orbits around the nucleus. Not all atoms of the same element are identical. Many elements have alternate forms called *isotopes* which have different numbers of neutrons. Figure 1 shows hydrogen and two of its isotopes. Some isotopes are more stable than others.

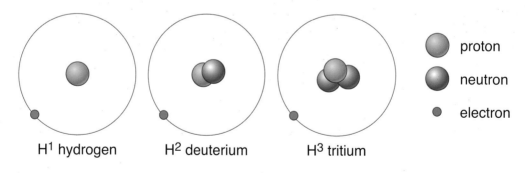

$H^1$ hydrogen    $H^2$ deuterium    $H^3$ tritium

proton
neutron
electron

Isotopes of hydrogen

**Figure 1**

The unstable isotopes of an element undergo *radioactive decay,* and in the process they become more stable atoms. Each type of isotope decays at a unique, predictable rate. The amount of time it takes for one half of a sample of atoms to decay is known as the isotopes' *half-life.* By analyzing the amount of the radioactive isotope remaining in a fossil or rock, scientists can use the half-life method to determine the age of the sample. In this activity, you will use beans that represent the imaginary element "beanium" to demonstrate the concept of radioactive decay.

## Time Required

45 minutes

## Materials

- dried beans, such as pinto beans (about 1/4 pound [lb.] (454 gram [g]))
- dried lentils (about 1/4 lb. [454 g])
- glue
- poster board
- graph paper
- science notebook

**Safety Note**    Please review and follow the safety guidelines at the beginning of this volume.

## Procedure

1.  In this activity, you will be working with the imaginary radioactive element beanium (dried beans) that decays into "lentilium" (lentils) after a half-life of 1,200 years. In other words, every 1,200 years, one-half of the atoms of the existing beanium turn into lentilium.

2.  Count out 128 atoms (beans) of beanium. This represents your original sample of atoms.

3.  Arrange the atoms in a circular shape and paste them onto the top left corner of the poster board. Label the circle of atoms as "original sample."

4.  Copy the data table into your science notebook, leaving room to extend it.

5. Calculate how many atoms of beanium will have decomposed into lentilium after 1,200 years. Record this amount on the data table.

6. Count out the appropriate number of beans and lentils to represent this sample.

7. Arrange the beans and lentils from step 6 into a circular shape and paste them next to the original sample on the poster board. Label this sample "1,200 years."

8. Using the number of beanium atoms remaining after 1,200 years, calculate the number of beanium atoms that will turn into lentilium after an additional 1,200 years. Record this number on the data table. Under "number of years passed," give the total number for two 1,200-year half-lives—2,400 years.

9. Count out the appropriate number of beans and lentils to represent this sample.

10. Arrange the beans and lentils from the newly counted sample into a circular shape and paste them to the poster board. Label this sample "2,400 years."

11. Repeat steps 8 through 10 until only one atom of beanium remains in the sample. Label each sample with the total number of years passed (3,600, 4,800, 6,000, and so forth), and record your findings on the data table. (If necessary, you can extend the data table.)

## Analysis

1. How many half-lives did your sample of beanium go through until the sample had decomposed to a single atom? How many years did that take?

2. If your final sample containing a single beanium atom were to go through another period of 1,200 years, what would occur?

3. Create a bar graph for the results of this activity, where the length of each bar represents the number of beanium atoms remaining in the sample.

4. How do you think the decay of radioactive elements be used to determine the age of something such as a fossil?

5. If the half-life of element X is 895 years, how many atoms from a 560-atom sample of element X would remain after 3,580 years?

6. A sample of element X (with the same half-life of 895 years) is found to contain 420 atoms. If the original sample contained 6,720 atoms, what is the estimated age of the sample?

| Data Table | | | |
|---|---|---|---|
| Number of half-lives | Number of beanium atoms | Number of lentilium atoms | Number of years passed |
| 0 | 128 | 0 | 0 |
| 1 | | | 1,200 |
| 2 | | | |
| 3 | | | |
| 4 | | | |
| 5 | | | |
| 6 | | | |

## What's Going On?

Isotopes of atoms decay because they are not stable. Usually their instability is due to the ratio between positively charged protons and neutral neutrons in the nucleus of the atom. There are two types of decay that occur in radioactive isotopes: alpha and beta. Alpha decay takes place when the number of protons is too high, and repulsion occurs between oppositely charged subatomic particles. In alpha decay, the atom emits an *alpha particle*, which is essentially the same as the nucleus of a helium atom, containing two protons and two neutrons, as shown in Figure 2. This type of decay produces a new element with an *atomic number* that is decreased by 2 and a *mass number* that is decreased by 4 from the original element.

The second type, beta decay, involves the release of a *beta particle*, which is a modified electron. Beta decay occurs when the proton-neutron ratio within the atom creates instability. In order to regain stability, a neutron

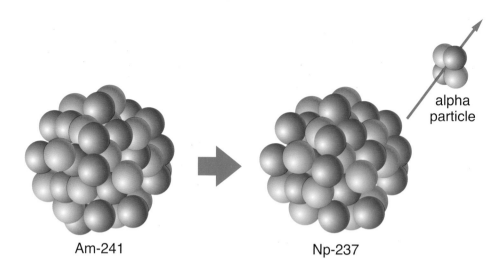

**Figure 2**

**Americium (Am) undergoes alpha decay, emitting an alpha particle and forming the more stable element neptunium.**

will transform into a proton and an electron. The electron is emitted as a beta particle, and the element is transformed into an element with an atomic number increased by one (see Figure 3). There are two other less-common forms of beta decay that occur when the proton-neutron ratio is too low. The first of these two types of decay is *positron emission*, where a proton emits a *positron,* a positive particle similar to an electron, and therefore becomes a neutron. The other type of beta decay is *electron capture*, where a proton essentially captures an electron from the surrounding electron cloud and becomes a neutron. In both of these types of beta decay, the atomic number decreases by one in the resulting atom.

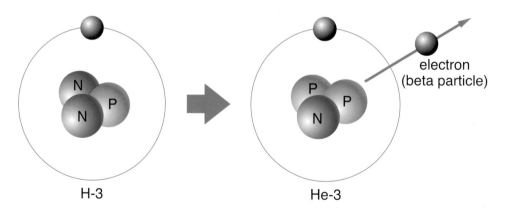

**Figure 3**

**Hydrogen 3, which has one proton (p) and two neutrons (n), undergoes beta decay to form helium 3, with two protons and one neutron.**

## Connections

Single atoms are so tiny that they cannot be seen even with the most advanced microscopes. However, atoms are not the smallest particles. They are made up of smaller subunits known as subatomic particles. For years, scientists thought that there were only three types of subatomic particles, positive protons and neutral neutrons in the nucleus, surrounded by negative electrons. However, scientists have discovered a variety of even smaller subatomic particles that play important roles influencing the characteristics of an atom. Among these are many varieties of particles known as *quarks* and *leptons*. Although not as well known as protons, neutrons, and electrons, these elementary particles are building blocks of every atom and help to determine how the atom reacts and how well the nucleus holds together.

*Neutrinos* are a type of lepton that do not have mass or a charge, but can influence the characteristics of an electron emitted during beta decay. In fact, in beta decay, neutrinos are thought to be given off alongside electrons. The emission of a neutrino decreases the strength of the radiation given off by electrons, which usually contain a great deal of energy. If an electron were to be emitted under normal circumstances, a photon of light, also known as a *gamma particle*, would be emitted. Gamma particles have very high energy and can cause damage to living organisms. However, thanks to neutrinos, beta decay does not emit particles that are capable of doing significant damage to their surroundings.

 **Want to Know More?**

See appendix for Our Findings.

## Further Reading

Brain, Marshall. "How Carbon-14 Dating Works," 2010. HowStuffWorks. Available online. URL: http://science.howstuffworks.com/carbon-142. htm. Accessed September 25, 2010. Brain explains the formula used to calculate the age of rocks and fossils using carbon 14.

Earth Science Australia. "Radioactive Dating," 2010. Available online. URL: http://earthsci.org/fossils/geotime/radate/radate.html. Accessed September 25, 2010. This Web site explains how numerical dates of rocks can be determined using the rubidium-strontium method.

Physics 2000. Available online. URL: http://www.edu/physics/2000/index.pl?Type=TOC. Accessed September 25, 2010. This Web site provides tutorials and interactive applets on dozens of physics topics, including half-life.

USGS. "Radiometric Time Scale," 2001. Available online. URL: http://pubs.usgs.gov/gip/geotime/radiometric.html. Accessed September 25, 2010. This Web site explains how half-lives are determined and discusses the "age equation," which relates radioactive decay and half-life to geologic time.

# 12. Wind Chill

## Topic

On a cool day, wind can reduce body temperature.

## Introduction

If you have ever seen of picture of a human or other warm-blooded animal taken with an infrared camera, you can easily see that the body radiates heat energy (see Figure 1). The body works constantly to keep its temperature stable. In humans, the average body temperature is 98.6 degrees Fahrenheit (°F) (37 degrees Celsius [°C]). Large skeletal muscles like the ones in your arms and legs are the primary heat producers in the body. As they contract, they use energy and generate heat.

The body loses heat in several ways. Some is given off through *conduction*, the transfer of heat energy from one substance to another through molecule-to-molecule contact. As molecules collide, energy moves from highly energetic particles to those that are in a lower energy state. Therefore, on cool days, heat moves from your warm body to the cool air.

In addition, convective energy transfer carries away some of your body heat. *Convection* is the movement of heat through circulating air currents.

 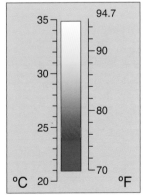

**Figure 1**

**A picture taken with an infrared camera shows the warmest and coldest areas of this dog.**

Convective heat transfer increases significantly with increasing air velocity. Thus, a person is cooled more when the air is moving. In cold weather, moving air can make the temperature seem significantly lower than it actually is. A measurement of the chilling effect of moving air is the *wind chill factor*. This measurement is not actually a temperature, but a comparison of the cooling effect of wind to the air temperature on a calm day. In this experiment, will see how wind affects the rate of heat transfer.

## Time Required

55 minutes

## Materials

- very warm water (from tap)
- shallow plastic bowl or small container (about the size of a large book)
- thermometer (Fahrenheit)
- anemometer
- small battery-powered fan
- aluminum foil
- calculator
- graph paper
- red pencil
- blue pencil
- clock or watch with a second hand
- science notebook

> **Safety Note**     Be careful when working with very warm water. Take care when using a fan near water. Please review and follow the safety guidelines at the beginning of this volume.

## Procedure

1.  Fill the container to a depth of about 0.5 inches (in.) (1.2 centimeters [cm]) with very warm water.

2.  Place the thermometer in the container so that the bulb is fully submerged. Prop the other end of the thermometer against the side of the container so that the temperature can be easily read.

3.  After the thermometer has been in place about 2 minutes (min), read the temperature and record it on Data Table 1 in the row labeled "initial" under the heading "Temperature (no fan)."

4.  Read and record the temperature every min for a total of 5 min.

5.  Repeat steps 1 through 4, but this time set up a small fan near one end of the plastic container (see Figure 2). Turn on the fan and record the temperatures in the last column of Data Table 1 under "Temperature (with fan)."

| Data Table 1 | | |
|---|---|---|
| **Time** | **Temperature (no fan)** | **Temperature (with fan)** |
| Initial | | |
| 1 min | | |
| 2 min | | |
| 3 min | | |
| 4 min | | |
| 5 min | | |

6.  Graph the experimental results recorded on the data table. On your graph, let the X-axis show time in min and the Y-axis show temperature. Use a red line to represent temperatures without the fan and a blue line to indicate the temperatures with the fan.

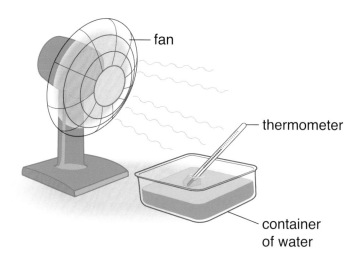

**Figure 2**

**Position the fan so that wind blows across the container of water.**

7. Use the anemometer to find the wind speed produced by the fan in miles per hour. Record the wind speed in your science notebook.

## Analysis

1. In this experiment, what represented your body?

2. In which case was heat lost faster: in the water without the fan or in the water with the fan?

3. On a chilly day, why does the wind make you feel colder than you would if the air were calm?

4. What would you expect to happen if you turned the fan up to a higher speed?

5. Data Table 2 shows wind chill factors if air temperature and wind speed are known. Based on your anemometer reading, what is the wind chill in a classroom that is 40°F (18°C)?

6. Calculate the wind chill factor of a 40°F (18°C) classroom using the following formula:

   $T_{we}(°F) = 35.74 + 0.6215T − 35.75 (V^{0.16}) + 0.4275T (Y^{0.16})$

   where $T_{wc}$ is wind chill, V is the wind speed (miles per hour), and T is the temperature (°F)

7. How close is your calculation to the value on the chart? What might have caused any differences?

| Temp- erature (°F) | Wind (mph) | | | | | | | | | | | |
|---|---|---|---|---|---|---|---|---|---|---|---|---|
| **Data Table 2** | | | | | | | | | | | | |
| calm | 5 | 10 | 15 | 20 | 25 | 30 | 35 | 40 | 45 | 50 | 55 | 60 |
| 40 | 36 | 34 | 32 | 30 | 29 | 28 | 28 | 27 | 26 | 26 | 25 | 25 |
| 35 | 31 | 27 | 25 | 24 | 23 | 22 | 21 | 20 | 19 | 19 | 18 | 17 |
| 30 | 25 | 21 | 19 | 17 | 16 | 15 | 14 | 13 | 12 | 12 | 11 | 10 |
| 25 | 19 | 15 | 13 | 11 | 9 | 8 | 7 | 6 | 5 | 4 | 4 | 3 |
| 20 | 13 | 9 | 6 | 4 | 3 | 1 | 0 | -1 | -2 | -3 | -3 | -4 |
| 15 | 7 | 3 | 0 | -2 | -4 | -5 | -7 | -8 | -9 | -10 | -11 | -11 |
| 10 | 1 | -4 | -7 | -9 | -11 | -12 | -14 | -15 | -16 | -17 | -18 | -19 |
| 5 | -5 | -10 | -13 | -15 | -17 | -19 | -21 | -22 | -23 | -24 | -25 | -26 |
| 0 | -11 | -16 | -19 | -22 | -24 | -26 | -27 | -29 | -30 | -31 | -32 | -33 |
| -5 | -16 | -22 | -26 | -29 | -31 | -33 | -34 | -36 | -37 | -38 | -39 | -40 |
| -10 | -22 | -28 | -32 | -35 | -37 | -39 | -41 | -43 | -44 | -45 | -46 | -48 |
| -15 | -28 | -35 | -39 | -42 | -44 | -46 | -48 | -50 | -51 | -52 | -54 | -55 |
| -20 | -34 | -41 | -45 | -48 | -51 | -53 | -55 | -57 | -58 | -60 | -61 | -62 |
| -25 | -40 | -47 | -51 | -55 | -58 | -60 | -62 | -64 | -65 | -67 | -68 | -69 |
| -30 | -46 | -53 | -58 | -61 | -64 | -67 | -69 | -71 | -72 | -74 | -75 | -76 |
| -35 | -52 | -59 | -64 | -68 | -71 | -73 | -76 | -78 | -79 | -81 | -82 | -84 |
| -40 | -57 | -66 | -71 | -74 | -78 | -80 | -82 | -84 | -86 | -88 | -89 | -91 |
| -45 | -63 | -72 | -77 | -81 | -84 | -87 | -89 | -91 | -93 | -95 | -97 | -98 |

## What's Going On?

In this experiment, you measured heat loss in a shallow container of warm water and compared it to heat loss when the same container was exposed to wind. The warm water represented the body of a living thing. You found that without wind, heat loss was relatively slow; but with the wind created by a fan, heat was dissipated much more quickly. If you had done this experiment outdoors on a cold day, heat loss in both cases would have been a little faster.

The wind chill factor is a reflection of how fast the wind draws heat out of the body, reducing the core body temperature. For this reason, wind makes us feel colder than the actual temperature. If the temperature is 35°F (1.6°C) and the wind is blowing at 10 mph, the temperature feels like it is 27°F (-2.7°C). Wind chill has little effect on inanimate objects. Even if the wind makes the temperature feel like it is 27°F (-2.7°C), water will not freeze until the temperature actually drops below freezing.

## Connections

A low wind chill increases one's risk of becoming too cold, leading to frostbite or hypothermia. *Frostbite* usually occurs in the fingers, toes, nose, and ears because the body protects the vital organs in cold weather by reducing circulation to extremities. Without the warmth of the blood, tissues that are exposed to cold weather are damaged when water in the tissues freezes, breaking open cells and killing them. The damaged tissue is said to have suffered frostbite. Symptoms of frostbite include numbness and pale color in the affected area. Frostbite can be a very serious condition; in some cases damaged tissue has to be removed. If you think that a person is suffering from frostbite, seek medical help immediately. If none is available, immerse the affected body part in comfortably warm, not hot, water. If warm water is not available, place the affected area against warm skin. For example, put your hands in your arm pits to warm them. Do not rub the affected area because this can cause more damage.

The same conditions that cause frostbite can also cause *hypothermia*, which is more dangerous. In hypothermia, the body temperature is abnormally low because heat is being lost faster than the body can generate it and the core temperature falls below 95°F (35°C). You might suspect that someone is hypothermic if they have uncontrollable shivering or seem disoriented, confused, or exhausted. As with frostbite, seek medical help. If clothing is wet, remove it and cover the person's body, not just their arms and legs, with blankets or coats. Try to get him or her indoors and provide something warm to drink that does not contain alcohol.

## Want to Know More?

See appendix for Our Findings.

## Further Reading

Air Sports Net. "Wind Chill Map for the United States." Available online. URL: http://www.usairnet.com/weather/maps/current/wind-chill/. Accessed October 2, 2010. This Web site has a map of the United States that is dedicated to posting wind chill temperatures.

"How Does the Windchill Factor Work?" 2010. HowStuffWorks. Available online. URL: http://science.howstuffworks.com/question70.htm. Accessed October 2, 2010. This articles explains how wind chill affects animate and inanimate objects.

Office of the Federal Coordinator for Meteorological Services and Supporting Research (OFCM). "Report on Wind Chill Temperature and Extreme Heat Indices: Evaluation and Improvement Projects," 2003. Available online. URL: http://www.ofcm.gov/jagti/r19-ti-plan/pdf/entire_r19_ti.pdf. Accessed October 2, 2010. This report for the advanced student details the history of wind chill calculation and explains why and how wind chill indices have been upgraded.

# 13. Relative Humidity

## Topic

Relative humidity can be measured with a simple psychrometer.

## Introduction

When you check with your local weather station, what kind of information do you want? You could be interested in the temperature or a forecast of precipitation. In warm months, you might also want to know the *humidity*, the amount of moisture in the air. *Meteorologists* usually report the *relative humidity*, a measurement of the amount of water vapor in the air compared to the maximum amount of water vapor that the air could hold at that temperature. Relative humidity is expressed as a percentage. When the relative humidity is 100 percent, the air is holding the maximum amount of water. When the weather is warm and relative humidity is high, many people find that the air feels sticky or muggy.

Relative humidity is influenced by air temperature. If the air is warm and dry, water can evaporate easily and enter air as a vapor. On the other hand, when air is cool and moist, air is already holding a lot of water vapor and so cannot take on much more. At every temperature, there is an upper limit to the amount of water vapor the air can hold. At 86 degrees Fahrenheit (86°F) (30 degrees Celsius [30°C]), a cubic meter (m³) of air can hold 30 grams (g) of water vapor. If the temperature drops to 69°F (20°C), the air can only hold 17 g and at 50°F (10°C) it can hold 9 g. The amount of relative humidity in air can be calculated with the formula:

$$\text{percent relative humidity} = \frac{\text{amount water actually in air}}{\text{maximum amount water vapor air can hold at that temperature}}$$

Relative humidity can be measured with an instrument called a *psychrometer*, a type of *hygrometer*. In this experiment, you will make a simple psychrometer and use it to measure relative humidity in the classroom and outdoors.

## Time Required

55 minutes

## Materials

- ⊷ 2 Celsius thermometers
- ⊷ small square of gauze (about the size of a playing card)
- ⊷ 3 rubber bands
- ⊷ small bowl or beaker half-filled with water (at room temperature)
- ⊷ scissors
- ⊷ pint (pt) milk carton (clean and unfolded on top)
- ⊷ small piece of cardboard
- ⊷ scalpel or knife
- ⊷ access to an outdoor area
- ⊷ science notebook

**Safety Note** Take care when working with the scalpel or knife. Please review and follow the safety guidelines at the beginning of this volume.

## Procedure

1. Place the two Celsius thermometers on your desk and leave them for about 2 minutes (min). Compare the thermometers to be sure that they read the same temperature. If they do not, get two thermometers that do.

2. Wrap the gauze around the bulb of one thermometer. If the gauze is too large, use the scissors to trim it. Secure the gauze to the thermometer using a rubber band.

3. Dip the bulb and gauze of this thermometer into the bowl or beaker of water until the gauze is saturated.

4. Using a scalpel or knife, punch a small hole in one side of the milk carton about 1 inch (in.) (2.5 centimeters [cm]) from the bottom of the carton.

5.  Push some of the gauze that is wrapped around the thermometer into the hole. Secure the thermometer against the carton using two rubber bands (see Figure 1). This is the wet-bulb thermometer.

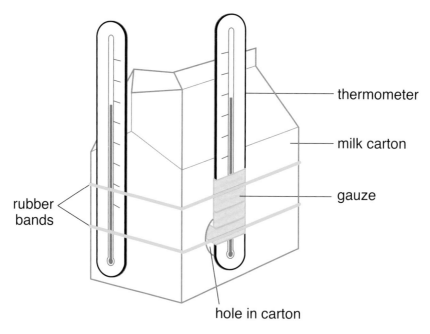

**Figure 1**

6.  On another side of the milk carton, slide the dry-bulb thermometer under the two rubber bands to secure it to the carton.

7.  Pour water into the carton so that is just touches the gauze. The purpose of the water is to keep the gauze wet.

8.  Place the carton and thermometers on your desk and use the piece of cardboard to fan the thermometers until the wet-bulb temperature stops going down. Read the temperature of both thermometers. Record the temperatures on Data Table 1 under "Location 1."

9.  Subtract the wet-bulb temperature from the dry-bulb temperature and record the difference on Data Table 1.

10. Read the relative humidity on Data Table 2. Find the dry-bulb readings in the left-hand column. In the row across the top of the table, find the temperature difference between the wet and dry bulbs. Find the point where this column intercepts the row of the dry-bulb reading. This is the relative humidity of location 1 expressed as a percentage.

11. Follow your teacher to an outdoor location. Place your psychrometer on the ground and use the piece of cardboard to fan the thermometer until the wet bulb temperature stops going down. Then repeat steps 8 through 10 and record the information on Data Table 1.

## Data Table 1

| | Location 1 | Location 2 |
|---|---|---|
| Dry-bulb temperature | | |
| Wet-bulb temperature | | |
| Difference in dry- and wet-bulb temperatures | | |
| Relative humidity | | |

## Data Table 2: Relative Humidity

| Dry bulb (°C) | Number of degrees difference between the wet- and dry-bulb readings (°C) | | | | | | | | | |
|---|---|---|---|---|---|---|---|---|---|---|
| | 1 | 2 | 3 | 4 | 5 | 6 | 7 | 8 | 8 | 10 |
| 10 | 88 | 77 | 66 | 56 | 45 | 35 | 26 | 16 | 7 | — |
| 11 | 89 | 78 | 67 | 57 | 47 | 38 | 28 | 19 | 11 | 2 |
| 12 | 89 | 79 | 68 | 59 | 49 | 40 | 31 | 22 | 14 | 5 |
| 13 | 89 | 79 | 69 | 60 | 51 | 42 | 33 | 25 | 16 | 9 |
| 14 | 90 | 80 | 70 | 61 | 52 | 43 | 35 | 27 | 19 | 11 |
| 15 | 90 | 80 | 71 | 62 | 54 | 45 | 37 | 29 | 22 | 14 |
| 16 | 90 | 81 | 72 | 63 | 55 | 47 | 39 | 31 | 24 | 17 |
| 17 | 91 | 82 | 73 | 64 | 56 | 48 | 41 | 33 | 26 | 19 |
| 18 | 91 | 82 | 73 | 65 | 57 | 50 | 42 | 35 | 28 | 21 |
| 19 | 91 | 82 | 74 | 66 | 58 | 51 | 44 | 37 | 30 | 24 |
| 20 | 91 | 83 | 75 | 67 | 59 | 52 | 45 | 38 | 32 | 26 |
| 21 | 91 | 83 | 75 | 68 | 60 | 53 | 47 | 40 | 34 | 27 |
| 22 | 91 | 84 | 76 | 69 | 61 | 54 | 48 | 41 | 35 | 29 |
| 23 | 92 | 84 | 77 | 69 | 62 | 56 | 49 | 43 | 37 | 31 |
| 24 | 92 | 84 | 77 | 70 | 63 | 57 | 50 | 44 | 38 | 32 |
| 25 | 92 | 85 | 77 | 71 | 64 | 57 | 51 | 45 | 40 | 34 |
| 26 | 92 | 85 | 78 | 71 | 65 | 58 | 52 | 46 | 41 | 35 |
| 27 | 93 | 85 | 78 | 72 | 65 | 59 | 53 | 47 | 42 | 37 |
| 28 | 93 | 86 | 79 | 72 | 66 | 60 | 54 | 49 | 43 | 38 |
| 29 | 93 | 86 | 79 | 73 | 67 | 61 | 55 | 50 | 44 | 39 |
| 30 | 93 | 86 | 80 | 73 | 67 | 61 | 56 | 50 | 45 | 40 |
| 31 | 93 | 86 | 80 | 74 | 68 | 62 | 57 | 51 | 46 | 41 |
| 32 | 93 | 87 | 80 | 74 | 68 | 63 | 57 | 52 | 47 | 42 |
| 33 | 93 | 87 | 81 | 75 | 69 | 63 | 58 | 53 | 48 | 43 |
| 34 | 93 | 87 | 81 | 75 | 69 | 64 | 59 | 54 | 49 | 44 |

## Analysis

1.  As you fanned the thermometers, which one showed the greatest change in temperature? Offer an explanation for this.

2.  In which location was the relative humidity the highest, indoors or outdoors?

3.  If you were to measure the outdoor relative humidity every hour from morning to evening, what do you think you would you find?

4.  Sweat is a cooling mechanism. As sweat evaporates, it removes heat from the body. In which situation would sweat be less able to evaporate, when relative humidity is high or when it is low. Why?

5.  If the difference between the wet- and dry-bulb thermometer temperatures is large, would you expect the relative humidity to be high or low? Explain your reasoning.

## What's Going On?

In this experiment, you built a wet- and dry-bulb psychrometer and used it to measure relative humidity in two locations. The principle behind the psychrometer is simple. When the relative humidity in air is low, water vapor easily evaporates from the wet-bulb thermometer, causing a significant drop in temperature. By calculating the difference in the temperature of the two thermometers and knowing air temperature, one can examine a table that shows relative humidity. On this table, you can see that the higher the temperature, the higher the relative humidity. It also shows that the greater the difference in the temperatures of the two thermometers, the higher the relative humidity.

There is an old saying that helps explain why warm muggy weather makes you uncomfortable: "It's not the heat; it's the humidity." An afternoon air temperature of 90°F (32°C) feels significantly different in Arizona, where relatively humidity is low, than it does in Mississippi, where the humidity is high. The relative humidity map for a day in July is shown in Figure 2. Notice the differences in the southeast and southwest.

## Connections

*Dew point* and relative humidity are often reported together because the measurements are related. Of the two, dew point gives a better indication of how much water vapor (humidity) is in the air. Relative humidity tells you how much water vapor the air contains compared to the maximum amount it could contain at that temperature. As temperature increases,

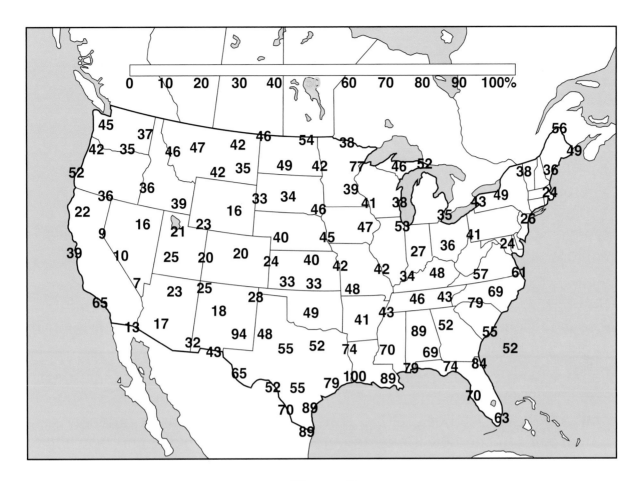

## Figure 2

### Typical relative humidity across the continental United States in July

the relative humidity decreases, even though the amount of water vapor in the air is unchanged. Dew point is the temperature to which air must be cooled for saturation to occur, assuming no change in pressure or moisture in the air. Saturated air is holding the maximum amount of water vapor; any drop in temperature will cause the water vapor to condense, or form dew. When relative humidity is high, the dew point is close to the current air temperature. If the relative humidity is 100 percent, the air is saturated with water and the dew point equals the current air temperature.

When the dew point is between 60°F (15.5°C) and 70°F (21°C), the air feels humid to most people. A dew point above 70°F (21°C) is extremely humid and sticky. In the United States, the dew point rarely exceeds 80°F (26.6°C). A record-breaking dew point of 95°F (35°C) was recorded in Dhahran, Saudi Arabia, on July 8, 2003. The temperature was 108°F (42.2°C), producing a *heat index* of 172°F (77.7°C). Heat index, also known as the felt air temperature, calculated from the actual temperature and the dew point, tells you how hot the air actually feels.

## Want to Know More?

See appendix for Our Findings.

## Further Reading

HyperPhysics. "Relative Humidity." Available online. URL: http://
hyperphysics.phy-astr.gsu.edu/hbase/kinetic/relhum.html. Accessed
October 2, 2010. Hosted by the department of physics and astronomy at
Georgia State University, this Web site explains how to calculate relative
humidity and relate the calculation to dew point.

Weather Central. "Current Relative Humidity," July 2010. Available online.
URL: http://www.weathercentral.com/weather/maps/us/humidity.html.
Accessed October 2, 2010. This Web site provides a daily map on relative
humidity in the United States.

Weather Wise. "Relative Humidity in the Winter and Summer," April 2010.
Available online. URL: http://itg1.meteor.wisc.edu/wxwise/relhum/rhac.
html. Accessed October 2, 2010. This applet lets you adjust outdoor
temperature to see how it affects outdoor relative humidity and dew point
as well as the indoor temperature and relative humidity.

# 14. Tracking a Hurricane

## Topic

By tracking hurricanes, meteorologists can learn about the characteristics and behavior of these storms.

## Introduction

A *hurricane* is a gigantic storm that may be hundreds of miles wide with winds reaching 200 miles per hour (mph) (174 knots [k]). The prime hurricane season in the Atlantic Ocean is June 1 to November 30, with most storms in the fall. In the eastern Pacific, the season extends from May 15 to November 30. For a hurricane to develop, conditions in the ocean and atmosphere must be just right.

A hurricane begins as a cluster of thunderstorms over a warm ocean in a region of high *humidity*. When the air is very humid, the amount of evaporation in clouds is relatively low, a condition that causes a lot of *precipitation*.

These circumstances take advantage of the available *latent heat*, energy released when a substance like water changes state. Latent heat helps to warm the atmosphere, causing the air to expand and push outward from the center of the storm. As air expands outward, the atmospheric pressure (measured in millibars [mbar]) above the ocean is reduced. Nearby air then moves into the low-pressure region at the center of the storm, creating an airflow that causes more warm, moist air to rise. The rising air cools and water in the air column condenses, forming clouds and releasing even more latent energy (see Figure 1). In this way, a cycle is set in motion that continues to build the storm.

Another important factor in hurricane development is the absence of strong *wind shear*, the amount of change in the speed or direction of wind with increasing altitude. As long as wind shear is weak, a storm can grow vertically, concentrating the energy of latent heat in centralized region. When wind shear is strong, the energy is spread over a large area, weakening the storm.

*Meteorologists* track hurricanes to gather information so they can predict the paths of future hurricanes. Not all hurricanes follow the same course,

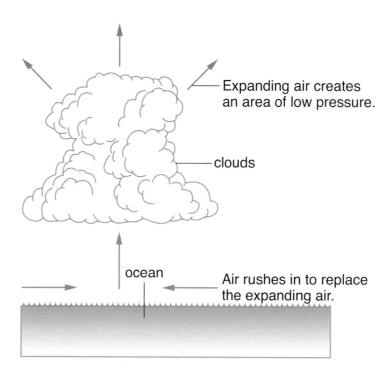

**Figure 1**

**Air moves into a low-pressure region at the center of a developing hurricane, creating an air current that causes warm, moist air to rise.**

but there are some patterns. Life-saving computer model projections of hurricane tracks and their intensity are partially based on analysis of past hurricane. In this experiment, you will track the path of Hurricane Katrina as it moved from the Bahamas to the United States. Hurricane Katrina was a deadly and costly hurricane that hit the coast of the Gulf of Mexico in 2005.

## Time Required

45 minutes

## Materials

- ● photocopy of Figure 2
- ● ruler
- ● access to the Internet
- ● science notebook

> **Safety Note** Please review and follow the safety guidelines at the beginning of this volume.

## Procedure

1. Examine Figure 2, a map of the Atlantic Ocean and Gulf of Mexico. The map shows lines of *latitude* and *longitude*. Latitude lines run from east to west and measure degrees north (°N) or south (°S) of the equator. Longitude lines run from north to south and measure degrees east (°E) or west (°W) of the *prime meridian*.

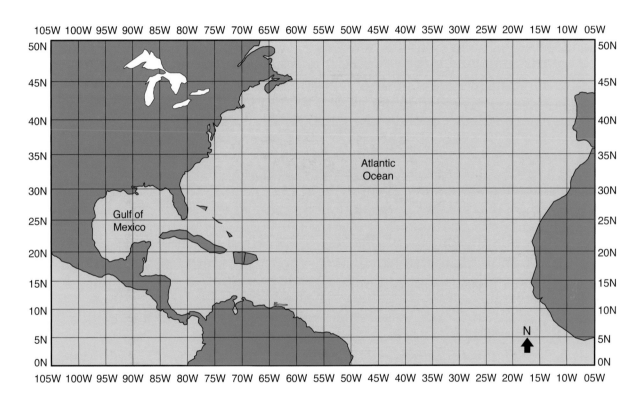

### Figure 2

### Atlantic basin in hurricane tracking chart

2. Data Table 1 lists some of the positions of Hurricane Katrina over a period of six days from August 23 to August 31, 2005. Each position is posted as an entry. Plot the position of entry 1 on the map in Figure 2. To do so:

   a. Notice that the latitude of entry 1 is 23.2 degrees. Find the latitude line that represents 20 degrees. Estimate 3.2 degrees above this line. Mark the position of 23.2 with a ruler.

    **b.** Entry 1 is at 75.5 degrees longitude. Find the longitude line that represents 75 degrees, then estimate the halfway point between 75 and 76. Mark the position 75.5 with one finger.

    **c.** Find the place where 23.2 degrees latitude and 75.5 degrees longitude intercept. Use your pencil to make a dot on the map at this point. Label this point as "1."

3. Repeat step 2 for all of the other entries on Data Table 1.

4. Connect all of the points with a line.

5. Answer Analysis questions 1 through 9.

6. On the Internet, visit the Katrina Graphic Archive at http://www. nhc.noaa.gov/archive/2005/KATRINA_graphics.shtml. On the left side of the page, under "Loop," select "Stop." Then use the forward arrow to advance the graphic one image at a time. Observe the graphic of Katrina's path two or three times, then answer Analysis questions 10 through 12.

## Analysis

1. What was the first land area to be hit by Hurricane Katrina?

2. At entry 6, where was the hurricane located?

3. What was the status of the storm: (a) when it entered the Bahamas? (b) when it left the Bahamas? (c) off the western coast of Florida? (d) just off the coast of Louisiana? (e) at landfall in Louisiana?

4. How did the status of the storm change as it moved from Louisiana to Tennessee?

5. What was the highest pressure in mbars during this storm? Where was the storm when the pressure was high?

6. What was the lowest pressure in mbars during this storm? Where was the storm when the pressure wave very low?

7. In general, during the period from August 23 to August 28, 2005: (a) how did wind speed change? (b) how did air pressure change?

8. Write a statement explaining the relationship between wind speed and air pressure from August 23 to August 28, 2005.

9. Where was the hurricane located when it began to lose energy?

10. How much time (in days) is covered by the animation of Katrina's path you viewed on the Internet? How does this compare to the time shown in the data table?

11.   How does the path of Hurricane Katrina in this animation compare to the path you drew on the photocopy of Figure 2?

12.   Why do you think that meteorologists study the paths of hurricanes?

## What's Going On?

A hurricane goes through several stages of development. It begins as a group of thunderstorms that come together at the right time and place to form a *tropical depression*, a rotating storm with winds from 23 to 39 mph (37 to 63 kmh). Within the storm, air pressure is relatively low and rotation around a central point and is not highly structured, so the storm may have a disorganized appearance.

If wind speed increases, reaching 39 to 73 mph (63 to 117 kph), and circulation becomes more organized, the event is classified as a *tropical storm* and given a name. High winds and heavy rains make tropical storms dangerous.

If air pressure continues to drop and winds reach 74 mph (119 kph), the weather event is called a *hurricane*. At this stage, the storm has a clear rotation around a central *eye*. Bordering the eye are the *eye walls*, regions of intense rain. The intensity of a hurricane is rated according to the Saffir-Simpson scale from 1 to 5, as shown on Data Table 2, with 1 as the weakest rating and 5 as the strongest. Hurricanes move slowly, traveling about 10 to 20 mph (16 to 32 kph). Once a hurricane reaches land or a region of cooler water, it begins to lose strength.

## Connections

Most hurricanes form between 5 to 15 degrees latitude north and south of equator. These types of storms never form over the equator because the *Coriolis effect,* which is needed to create the storm's spin, is weak there. The Coriolis effect (see Figure 3) is the apparent deflection of moving objects in the atmosphere to one side because the Earth is spinning underneath. In reality, the object is moving in a straight line; but because the Earth turns under it, the path of the object does not seem straight. In the Northern Hemisphere, the Coriolis force deflects objects to the right; in Southern Hemisphere, to the left.

| Data Table 1 | | | | | | | |
|---|---|---|---|---|---|---|---|
| Entry | Date (August 2005) | Time | Latitude (°N) | Longitude (°W) | Wind speed mph (k) | Pressure (mbar) | Status |
| 1 | 23 | 5 P.M. | 23.2 | 75.5 | 35 (30) | 1,007 | Tropical depression |
| 2 | 24 | 12 A.M. | 23.4 | 75.7 | 35 (30) | 1,007 | Tropical depression |
| 3 | 24 | 12 P.M. | 25.5 | 76.5 | 35 (30) | 1,006 | Tropical storm |
| 4 | 24 | 5 P.M. | 25.6 | 77.2 | 39 (45) | 1,002 | Tropical storm |
| 5 | 25 | 2 A.M. | 26.1 | 78.4 | 58 (50) | 1,000 | Tropical storm |
| 6 | 25 | 7 P.M. | 25.9 | 80.1 | 80 (70) | 985 | Hurricane 1 |
| 7 | 26 | 1 A.M. | 25.9 | 80.3 | 80 (70) | 983 | Hurricane 1 |
| 8 | 26 | 12 P.M. | 25.1 | 82.0 | 86 (75) | 979 | Hurricane 1 |
| 9 | 27 | 2 A.M. | 24.2 | 84.0 | 110 (96) | 963 | Hurricane 2 |
| 10 | 27 | 12 P.M. | 24.4 | 84.7 | 115 (100) | 942 | Hurricane 3 |
| 11 | 28 | 2 A.M. | 25.1 | 86.8 | 145 (126) | 935 | Hurricane 4 |
| 12 | 28 | 12 P.M. | 25.7 | 87.7 | 167 (145) | 909 | Hurricane 5 |
| 13 | 28 | 6 P.M. | 26.3 | 88.6 | 173 (150) | 902 | Hurricane 5 |
| 14 | 29 | 1 A.M. | 28.2 | 89.6 | 144 (125) | 913 | Hurricane 4 |
| 15 | 29 | 12 P.M. | 29.5 | 89.6 | 127 (110) | 923 | Hurricane 3 |
| 16 | 30 | 5 A.M. | 34.7 | 88.4 | 50 (43) | 961 | Tropical storm |
| 17 | 30 | 12 P.M. | 35.6 | 88 | 35 (30) | 985 | Tropical depression |
| 18 | 31 | 1 A.M. | 38.6 | 85.3 | 35 (30) | 994 | Storm |

| Data Table 2: Saffir-Simpson Hurricane Scale | |
|---|---|
| **Category** | **Wind speed mph (km/h)** |
| 5 | >156 (>250) |
| 4 | 131–155 (210-249) |
| 3 | 111–130 (178-209) |
| 2 | 96–110 (154-177) |
| 1 | 74–95 (119-153) |
| **Additional classifications** | |
| Tropical storm | 39–73 (63-117) |
| Tropical depression | 0–38 (0-62) |

## Want to Know More?

See appendix for Our Findings.

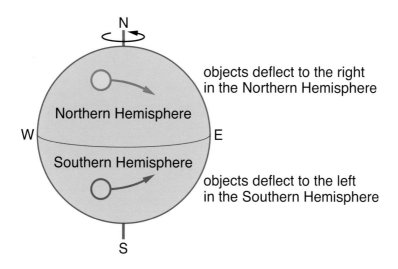

Figure 3

The spin of a hurricane is due to the Coriolis effect, which is caused by the Earth's rotation.

## Further Reading

Intellicast. "Active Track," 2010. Available online. URL: http://www.intellicast.com/Storm/Hurricane/Track.aspx. Accessed October 2, 2010. On this Web site, one can follow the daily progress of storms on maps that show satellite imagery.

National Weather Service. "National Hurricane Center," 2010. Available online. URL: http://www.nhc.noaa.gov/. Accessed October 2, 2010. The Web site is updated daily with data related to tropical depressions, storms, and hurricanes.

"The 11 Worst Hurricanes," South Florida *Sun Sentinel* 2010. Available online. URL: http://www.sun-sentinel.com/news/local/southflorida/sfl-aug2001hurricanehistory,0,637516.storygallery. Accessed October 2, 2010. This Web page describes the 11 worst hurricanes in Florida and provides links to other information on hurricanes.

# 15. Hailstone Formation

## Topic

Hailstones form in the atmosphere around nuclear particles under particular atmospheric conditions.

## Introduction

When you recall the last summer thunderstorm you witnessed, you may remember rain, wind, and frequent lightning strikes. Severe thunderstorms are the products of *cumulonimbus clouds*, dense clouds that are tall enough to extend through several layers of the atmosphere. Large cumulonimbus clouds can reach altitudes of 10 miles (mi) (16 kilometers [km]) or more in height. When atmospheric conditions are just right, these warm weather storms produce icy precipitation in the form of *hail*. These conditions include strong upward airflows and very cold temperatures in the atmosphere. Hailstones, individual lumps or balls of ice, are formed when *updrafts* lift water droplets up into regions where the air is below freezing; *downdrafts* then carry the frozen droplets back toward Earth. The stones can easily get caught in updrafts and downdrafts that cycle them up into cold air and back down into warmer regions (see Figure 1).

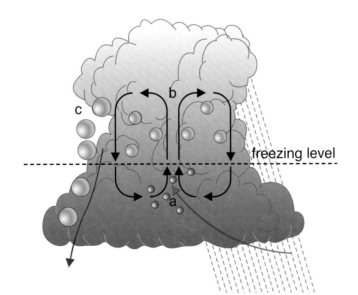

a. Raindrops are pulled up into the cloud by an updraft.

b. The water freezes and forms hail, which grow as it circulates up and down in the cloud.

c. When the hail is too large to be supported by the cloud, it falls to Earth.

**Figure 1**

**How hail forms**

Hailstones go through three stages of development. In the beginning, hailstones are small, white particles that resemble snow. At this stage they are known as *graupel* or *soft hail*. As they travel up and down in the atmosphere, the stones grow in size and are called *small hail*. These lumps of ice are dense, conical in shape, and semitransparent. Continued cycling in the atmosphere produces true hailstones, which can be as small as peas or as large as softballs. These balls of ice are made up of several alternating layers of clear ice and white or opaque ice (see Figure 2). Large hailstones have a lot of speed and mass, so they can be dangerous and cause serious property damage. In this experiment, you will find out what conditions are required to produce hail.

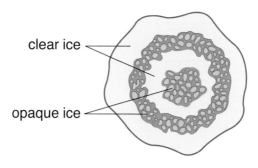

**Figure 2**

**A hailstone is made of alternating layers of clear and opaque ice.**

## Time Required

45 minutes

## Materials

- beaker (400 to 600 milliliters [ml])
- test tube
- thermometer
- crushed ice (about a cup [c])
- ice cream salt (about 1/4 c)
- stirring rod
- access to water
- paper towels
- test-tube brush

- liquid dishwashing detergent

- several small particles such as sand (a few grains), salt (a few grains), sugar (a few grains), half of a small, dried pea, or a tiny piece of bark

- science notebook

**Safety Note** **Please review and follow the safety guidelines at the beginning of this volume.**

## Procedure

1. Wash your test tube using a test-tube brush and a drop of detergent. Rinse the test tube, then dry with paper towels. Be sure that the inside surface is clean and free of any particles.

2. Fill the beaker about one-third full of water. Add salt to the water, stirring to mix, until no more will dissolve. (You may have some undissolved salt in the bottom of the beaker, which is fine.)

3. Add crushed ice to the water until the beaker is about two-thirds full.

4. Put the test tube in the beaker. Add cold water to the test tube until the levels of water in the test tube and beaker are about the same.

5. Place the thermometer in the beaker of ice water.

6. Gently stir the ice water with the stirring rod for about 10 minutes (min).

7. Read the temperature of the ice water. Record the temperature in your science notebook.

8. Observe the contents of the test tube and describe them as *frozen*, *partially frozen*, or *not frozen* in your science notebook.

9. Gently remove the test tube from the beaker without disturbing the contents. Drop one piece of ice into the test tube and observe. Describe what happens in your science notebook.

10. Repeat steps 1 through 9, but drop a different particle in the test tube. Compare the effects of the ice on the different particles.

## Analysis

1. What was the temperature of the water in the beaker?

2. What is the freezing point of water?

3.  Do you think that the water in the beaker and the water in the test tube is the same temperature? Explain your reasoning.

4.  In step 8, how did you describe the contents of the test tube?

5.  What happened when you dropped a piece of ice into the test tube? Explain why you think this happened.

6.  What other particle did you drop into a test tube? What happened with this particle?

7.  Based on the results of your experiment, why do you think the test tube had to be very clean?

8.  Based on the results of your experiment, what factors are necessary for hail to form?

## What's Going On?

In this experiment, you found that very cold water is not enough to produce an ice crystal. For ice to form, whether in a test tube or in the atmosphere, a small *condensation particle* or nucleus is required. Any small particle, even a few flakes of snow or a frozen water droplet, will serve the purpose. In some cases, pieces of dirt, broken sticks, or tiny bugs that are swept into the air by wind act as nuclei for hail.

Once a hailstone forms, it can increase in size. This enlargement can occur in either of two ways: wet growth or dry growth. In wet growth, a tiny piece of ice is suspended in a part of the atmosphere that is cold, but not supercold. The ice collides with a *supercooled* drop of water, water that is in the liquid state even though its temperature is below freezing. Instead of freezing to the ice immediately, the supercooled water spreads across the falling ice, freezing gradually. Because freezing occurs relatively slowly, any air bubbles dissolved in the water have time to escape, and the ice layer that forms is clear or transparent. In dry growth, the ice particle is in a region that is supercold. When it collides with a water droplet, freezing occurs immediately. Air bubbles are trapped in the ice, giving the layer a cloudy appearance.

Some hailstones are quite large. They gain layers by being repeatedly tossed up into the atmosphere. Every time the stones travel upward into cold air, they gain another layer of ice. One can tell how many times the hailstone has been lifted up into cold air at the peak of the storm by cutting it in half and counting the layers of ice. Eventually a hailstone becomes so large and heavy that the force of gravity pulling it down is stronger than the updraft in the thunderstorm.

## Connections

Hailstorms can be dangerous weather events, so meteorologists keep a close eye on severe thunderstorms. Visual inspection of a storm-producing cloud will not tell you whether or not it contains hail. However, weather radar can reveal the presence of hail inside a storm. Hail has more energy than rain, so it produces a red reflection on radar that helps meteorologists make their predictions (see Figure 3). Radar even makes it possible to predict the size of hailstorms within a cumulonimbus cloud.

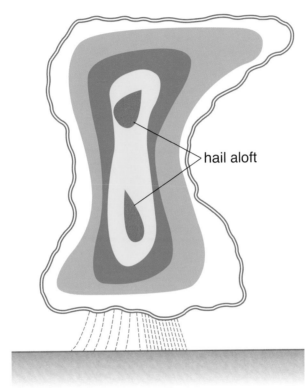

hail aloft

### Figure 3

**When viewed on weather radar, hail is red.**

You may have heard meteorologists refer to hail as "pea size" or "soft ball size." These descriptive terms make it easy to visualize the hailstones. You can translate the descriptive terms to actual sizes using the information on the data table.

The largest hailstone found in the United States fell in Aurora, Nebraska, on June 23, 2003. This record-breaking sphere was 7 in. (17.8 cm) wide and weighed almost one pound (lb) (2.2 kilograms [kg]). During the storm that spawned this gigantic stone, hail caused property damage in excess of $500,000 and crop damage across the county of $1 million.

Hailstones left craters in the ground that were 14 in. (35.6 cm) wide and 3 in. (7.6 cm) deep. This hail was part of a thunderstorm that also yielded tornados and floods.

| Data Table | |
|---|---|
| **Description of hail** | **Size** |
| Pea size | 0.25 inches (in.) (0.6 centimeters [cm]) |
| Marble size | 0.5 in. (1.3 cm) |
| Quarter size | 1.0 in. (2.5 cm) |
| Ping-Pong™ ball size | 1.5 in. (3.8 cm) |
| Golf ball size | 1.75 in. (4.4 cm) |
| Tennis ball size | 2.5 in. (6.4 cm) |
| Baseball size | 2.75 in. (7 cm) |
| Grapefruit size | 4.0 in. (10.2 cm) |
| Softball size | 4.5 in. (11.4 cm) |

## Want to Know More?

See appendix for Our Findings.

## Further Reading

Guyer, Jared L., and Rick Ewald. "Record Hail Event—Examination of the Aurora, Nebraska, Supercell of 22 June 2003." NOAA. Available online. URL: http://www.spc.noaa.gov/publications/guyer/aurora.pdf. Accessed October 2, 2010. This article, for the advanced student, explains the weather conditions that produced record-breaking hail in Nebraska.

Heidorn, Keith C. "Weather Phenomenon and Elements: Hail Formation," 2002. Available online. URL: http://www.islandnet.com/~see/weather/elements/hailform.htm. Accessed October 2, 2010. On this Web site, Heidorn, the "Weather Doctor," provides great photographs of hailstones and explains how they form.

Palmer, Chad. "Rising Air Creates Spring, Summer Ice," 2010. *USA Today*. Available online. URL: http://www.usatoday.com/weather/tg/whail/whail.htm. Accessed October 2, 2010. Palmer provides a simplified explanation of hail formation and the damage caused by hailstorms.

# 16. Speed of Evaporation

## Topic

Heat, light, and wind are some of the factors that affect the rate of evaporation.

## Introduction

Water is a unique compound in that its physical and chemical properties have shaped the Earth and the development of life. In the environment, water is constantly traveling through a path known as the *hydrologic cycle*, shown in Figure 1. As it circulates, water changes *phases*. The Sun's radiant energy causes water to evaporate and form water vapor in the air directly above the Earth's surface. This hot, moist surface air rises to higher altitudes. Temperatures are lower in the upper atmosphere, and

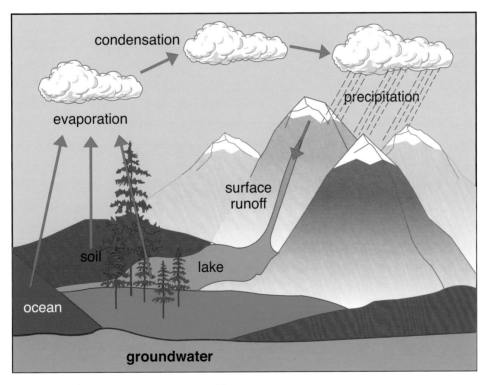

**Figure 1**

**The hydrologic cycle**

water vapor condenses to form clouds. Eventually clouds release the water as precipitation, which falls to Earth where it collects ground water reservoirs or runs off into streams, rivers, and eventually the ocean. Water vapor in the atmosphere is replenished by evaporation from surface water and *evapotranspiration* in plants.

Evaporation is a phase change that requires an input of energy. Known as the *latent heat of evaporation*, this energy helps individual water molecules escape from the *hydrogen bonds* that hold them together in the liquid form. Water molecules are capable of forming hydrogen bonds because they are *polar*. In a water molecule, the nucleus of the oxygen atom is much larger than the nuclei of the two hydrogen atoms. As a result, the electrons shared by these atoms spend most of their time on the oxygen end of the molecule. Consequently, the oxygen end has a slight negative charge and the hydrogen ends are slightly positive. Neighboring water molecules are attracted to each other very much like small bar magnets (see Figure 2). The bonds are not very strong, but powerful enough to slow evaporation.

It is impossible to know exactly how much water evaporates from the Earth's surface each year. Studies of the ocean's surface, the primary source of water for the atmosphere, indicate that the rate of evaporation is about 254 inches (in.) (100 centimeters [cm]) per year. The rate of evaporation over land, forest, or deserts would be less. Several factors account for the difference in regional evaporation rates. In this experiment, you will design your own procedure to compare the effect of three factors on the rate of evaporation: heat, light, and wind.

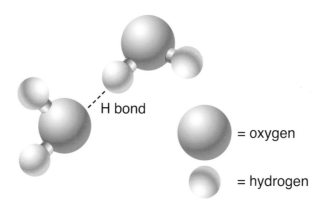

**Figure 2**

**Water molecules are described as polar because they have slight positive and negative charges on opposite ends. The attraction of two oppositely charged parts of water molecules forms a hydrogen bond.**

## Time Required

65 minutes

## Materials

- 2 Petri dishes
- 4 small sponges
- graduated cylinder
- clock with a second hand or stopwatch
- ring stand with ring attached
- electronic balance
- ruler
- electric fan
- lamp with bulb
- small electric space heater
- access to hot and cold water
- access to room temperature water
- plastic bags (sandwich size)
- paper clips
- string
- tape
- scissors
- science notebook

**Safety Note**   Take care when working with the space heater and fan. Do not use electrical devices near water. Please review and follow the safety guidelines at the beginning of this volume.

## Procedure

1. Your job is to work with two or three other students to design and perform an experiment that compares the effects of three factors on evaporation: heat, light, and wind.

2. You can use any of the supplies provided by your teacher, but you probably will not need to use all of them. If your group needs other items, discuss them with your teacher to see if they are available.

3. Before you conduct your experiment, decide exactly what you are going to do. Keep these points in mind:

   a. Set up a control that is not influenced by any of the factors you are testing. Use the control to find out the rate at which water evaporates (from a pan, sponge, or some other container) when it is not exposed to heat, light, or wind.

   b. Only test one factor at a time. For example, if you want to see how light affects the rate of evaporation, be sure that your experimental set-up is not exposed to heat and wind. Likewise, when you are testing the effect of heat, turn off the light and be sure that the set-up is not exposed to wind.

4. Write the steps you plan to take (your experimental procedure) and the materials you plan to use (materials list) on the data table. Show your procedure and materials list to the teacher. If you get teacher approval, proceed with your experiment. If not, modify your work and show it to your teacher again.

5. Once you have teacher approval, assemble the materials you need and begin your procedure.

6. As you carry out your experiment, collect your results on a data table of your own design.

## Analysis

1. Based on your experimental results, how is the rate of evaporation affected by (a) heat; (b) light; (c) wind.

2. What factors did you control in this experiment?

3. Based on what you have learned about water and evaporation, how do you think the following would affect evaporation:

   a. high humidity above water's surface

   b. water's surface area

4. If you want to conserve water, what is the best time of day to water your lawn? Explain your reasoning.

5. Would you need to water your garden more when the weather is windy or when it is calm? Why?

| Data Table | |
|---|---|
| **Your experimental procedure** | |
| **Your materials list** | |
| **Teacher's approval** | |

## What's Going On?

In the real world, several factors acting simultaneously affect the rate of evaporation. However, your assignment was to develop a method to isolate three of the factors and find out how each one affects evaporative rate. There are many ways to set up such an experiment. One method is to saturate a sponge with water then weigh it. The saturated sponge is then hung from a ring stand in a protected environment so that it is not exposed to wind, heat, or light. Every 15 minutes, the sponge is weighed to find out how much water has evaporated. The same setup can be used to expose a saturated sponge to the light of a lamp, heat from a small space heater, and wind produced by a fan.

In your procedure, you most likely found that heat, light, and moving air sped up the rate of evaporation. Molecules of water cannot evaporate unless they have enough *kinetic energy* to overcome the forces of attraction between individual water molecules. Generally, the rate of evaporation is slow because only a few particles at a liquid's surface possess the required energy. However, the addition of energy (either heat or light) to the system increases movement of the molecules. Water molecules that are moving fast are able to break free of the forces that hold them to other water molecules, and evaporation occurs.

Moving air speeds up evaporation because of factors related to the water and to space. As long as water molecules are held together by intermolecular bonds, evaporation does not occur. Wind breaks apart some of the bonds, making it possible for molecules to escape. The second factor has to do with the number of newly evaporated water molecules above the water. When evaporation occurs, gaseous water molecules are suspended just above the water's surface. As a result, there is very little room available to for more molecules, so evaporation slows. Wind moves these water vapor molecules out of the way, creating plenty of space for more. As a result, wind speeds up evaporation.

## Connections

The amount of water vapor in the air influences *weather*, what you experience outside on a day-to-day basis, and *climate*, the average weather over a long period of time. Water vapor is related to fog and cloud formation, humidity, precipitation, and severe weather. Recent research on weather and climate has focused on *global warming*, an increase in Earth's average surface temperature. Global warming is caused by an increase in the concentration of *greenhouses gases*, a group of compounds that trap heat near the planet's surface that include carbon dioxide, methane, and water vapor (see Figure 3). Increased levels of carbon dioxide are caused by the combustion of fossil fuels in cars, power plants, and industries. Until recently, carbon dioxide has been identified as the primary culprit in the global warming problem. However, recent studies by Susan Solomon with the U.S. National Oceanic and Atmospheric Administration (NOAA) suggest that almost one-third of global warming in the 1990s was caused by an increase in water vapor in the upper atmosphere. After 2000, water vapor levels dropped, and the rate of global warming decreased slightly, strengthening the argument. Solomon's findings make it clear that global warming is a complex problem that is influenced by multiple factors in the environment.

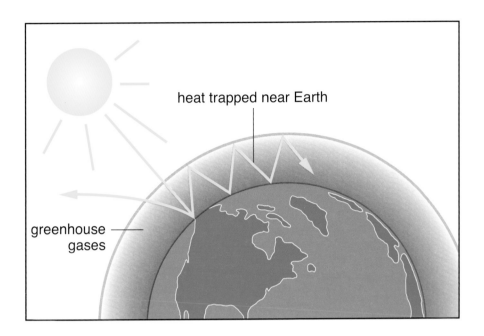

## Figure 3

**The greenhouse effect warms the Earth. Some of the sunlight that strikes Earth is reflected from the surface and trapped by a layer of greenhouse gases, including carbon dioxide and water vapor.**

 **Want to Know More?**

See appendix for Our Findings.

## Further Reading

Adam, David. "Water Vapour Caused One-third of Global Warming in 1990s, Study Reveals," *Guardian*, January 29, 2010. Available online. URL: http://www.guardian.co.uk/environment/2010/jan/29/water-vapour-climate-change. Accessed October 2, 2010. Adams explains how recent research on water vapor in the atmosphere has provided new insights into the causes of global warming in this article.

Melville, Kate. "The Role of Water Vapor in Climate Change," October 4, 1999. *Science a GoGo*. Available online. URL: http://www.scienceagogo.

com/news/19990904032112data_trunc_sys.shtml. Accessed October 2, 2010. In this article, Melville discusses the opinions of three scientists who have linked increasing levels of water vapor in the air to global warming.

USGS. "Summary of the Water Cycle," April 14, 2010. Available online. URL: http://ga.water.usgs.gov/edu/watercyclesummary.html. Accessed October 2, 2010. This Web site discusses all parts of the water cycle, including evaporation, in detail.

# 17. Color Filters on Telescopes

## Topic

Color filters on telescopes can improve images of the Moon, the planets, and other heavenly bodies.

## Introduction

Astronomers rely on telescopes to view objects in space. Objects seen through telescopes either produce light or reflect light from the Sun or other stars. Telescopes gather and focus the light to form the image that astronomers view. Often, astronomers add *color filters,* which are especially useful when observing the planets. Filters, used singly or in groups, provide more information than the telescope alone. Color filters help reduce *glare* from bright planets like Jupiter. Reducing glare is helpful because the Sun's reflected light can produce so much glare that it is impossible to make out details on the planets' surface. In addition, color filters enhance *contrast*, bringing features into view that may not be obvious with normal color. As contrast improves, astronomers are able to see more small details.

Color filters are available in dozens of shades, and they can be used in combinations. Figure 1 shows the basic colors used by many astronomers. When using color filters, one must remember that the objects are not being seen as they really are. No single filter gives completely accurate representations, but data gathered from using each of the filters provides useful information. The goal is to find a filter, or combination of filters, that enhances points of interest and mutes features that might be distracting. For example, if an astronomer is viewing the Crab *nebula*, a huge cloud of hot gas and dust in space, the blue filter might be used to study the central section, which is very hot. The outer, gaseous regions are produced by hydrogen and have a red color, so a red filter would bring out this region. Oxygen gas produces a green glow and green filters can help locate oxygen. A yellow filter can improve the view of filament structures in the center of the nebula. In this activity, you will build a color filter wheel and use it to observe objects to see how filters improve analysis.

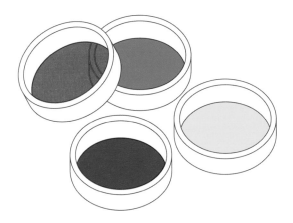

**Figure 1**

Red, green, blue, and yellow are four color filters commonly used on telescopes.

## Time Required

45 minutes

## Materials

- ➥ 2 pieces of card stock (12 by 12 inches [in]) (30.48 by 30.48 centimeters [cm])
- ➥ red cellophane (about the size of a small index card)
- ➥ blue cellophane (about the size of a small index card)
- ➥ yellow cellophane (about the size of a small index card)
- ➥ green cellophane (about the size of a small index card)
- ➥ prong paper file fastener
- ➥ X-Acto™ knife
- ➥ tape
- ➥ scissors

**Safety Note**     Take care when using the X-Acto™ knife. Please review and follow all safety guidelines at the beginning of this volume.

## Procedure

1.  Cut the two pieces of card stock into circles, each about the size of a dinner plate.

2.  Label the back of one circle "A"; label the back of the other "B."

3.  Use the X-Acto™ knife to cut out a portion of circle A as shown in Figure 2a. This cutout area will serve as a window on your color filter wheel.

4.  The piece you cut out will be used as a pattern. Trace the pattern on circle B four times, as shown in Figure 2b.

5.  Tape a small piece of blue cellophane to the back of circle B so that it covers one of the cutouts.

6.  Tape a small piece of red cellophane over another cutout on circle B.

7.  Tape a small piece of green cellophane over another cutout on circle B.

8.  Tape a small piece of yellow cellophane over the last cutout on circle B. When all four pieces of cellophane are in place, circle B should resemble Figure 2c.

9.  Use the X-Acto™ knife to cut a hole in the center of both circles.

10. Place circle A on top of circle B. Push the fastener through the holes to join the two circles. You have made a color filter wheel.

11. Examine Figure 3 and predict how it would appear if viewed through the yellow filter. Record your prediction in your science notebook.

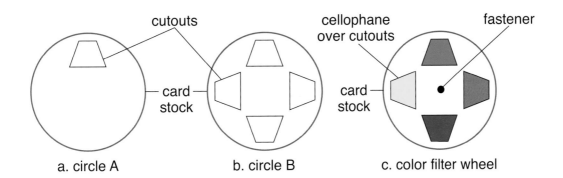

a. circle A            b. circle B            c. color filter wheel

**Figure 2**

**Construct the color filter wheel from two circular pieces of card stock and four colors of cellophane.**

**Figure 3**

**When viewed through color filters, certain features in this picture will be accentuated while others are muted.**

12. Turn the wheel so that the yellow cellophane is in the window and observe Figure 3. Describe its appearance in your science notebook.

13. Repeat steps 12 and 13 with each of the other filters.

14. Observe different objects around the classroom with all four filters. Make notes in your science notebook about the appearance of the objects through the filters.

## Analysis

1. Based on what you already know about light, what are the colors of white light?

2. Based on your previous knowledge of color, why does grass appear green?

3. Why do astronomers use color filters on their telescopes?

4. Were the predictions you made in step 11 accurate?

5. When the yellow filter is in place, what color(s) are visible in the image or object you are observing? Why?

## What's Going On?

What we call white light is the part of the *electromagnetic spectrum* that can be perceived by the human eye. When white light passes through a *prism*, it is broken down into its component colors. Each color of the spectrum is characterized by a *wavelength*. On the red end of the spectrum, wavelengths are long. They decrease in size as you move toward the violet end (see Figure 4).

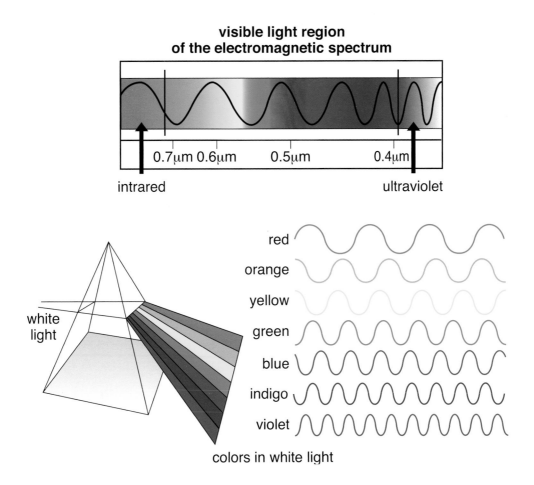

**visible light region
of the electromagnetic spectrum**

0.7μm 0.6μm    0.5μm      0.4μm

intrared                              ultraviolet

white
light

red
orange
yellow
green
blue
indigo
violet

colors in white light

## Figure 4

**White light is made up of many different colors, each with a
characteristic wavelength.**

The color filters that you constructed change the way you see images
because they block some wavelengths but let others be transmitted.
When you viewed Figure 3 through the filters, all of the colors were
blocked except for the one characteristic color of the filter. For example,
the yellow filter brought out the yellow details in the picture; all of
the other colored objects appeared gray or colorless. The same thing
happened with the green filter; only green wavelength passed through the
filter to your eyes.

Astronomers favor filters in general because they improve the contrast
of images in the telescope. Contrast is the difference in brightness in
different regions of the image. Glare due to reflected sunlight is a problem
when viewing the Moon and some of the planets. Filters help by reducing
the intensity of the glare and by increasing the contrast between features
in the image.

## Connections

Astronomers take advantage of color filters to improve the views of stars, planets, galaxies, and nebulae. When viewing planets, filters are especially important. Without a filter, Mars appears to be orange but details are not visible. With red and orange filters on the telescope, details on the surface are enhanced. If an astronomer wants to study the bluish clouds around Mars, green, blue, and violet filters are helpful. A light yellow filter enhances the *maria*, large dark regions, on this planet. Yellow also brings out the polar ice caps and desert regions by increasing contrast.

Yellow filters are also useful when viewing the belts on Jupiter because they increase the contrast between individual bands. The *Great Red Spot* is a huge storm on Jupiter, about three times the size of Earth, that has been active on the planet's surface for at least 300 years. To analyze the Great Red Spot, an astronomer might select a blue filter, which makes the region more distinct. Yellow filters darken the *blue festoons*, huge clouds that have fingerlike projections, near the equator of Jupiter. A red filter sharpens the contrast between surface features and clouds on the planet.

## Want to Know More?

See appendix for Our Findings.

## Further Reading

Beish, Jeff. "A Guide to Color Filters," Scope City Learning Center. Available online. URL: http://www.scopecity.com/A-Guide-to-Color-Filters. cfm?pn=A+Guide+to+Color+Filters. Accessed October 2, 2010. Beish, a former member of the Association of Lunar and Planetary Observers, Mars Section, explains how color filters in telescope improve viewing.

Carroll, Susan. "Astronomy for Everyone: The Use of Filters," 2010. SciAstro.net. Available online. URL: http://sciastro.net/members/ portia.php/2009/01/31/g-the-use-of-filters. Accessed October 2, 2010. SciAstro.net is a network of amateur astronomers who share information. This Web page discusses color filters and their uses.

NASA. "The Electromagnetic Spectrum," June 11, 2008. Available online. URL: http://imagine.gsfc.nasa.gov/docs/science/know_l1/ emspectrum.html. Accessed October 2, 2010. This Web page explains the electromagnetic spectrum and discusses how various telescopes use different regions of the spectrum to gather data from space.

# 18. Making a Planisphere

## Topic

A planisphere can be constructed to help identify stars and constellations.

## Introduction

If you go outside on a clear autumn night and observe the sky, you may see familiar *constellations* such as Aquarius and Pegasus. However, a return trip to the same place in the spring might give you a surprise: the constellations would not be in the same locations. Some of them might not even be visible. Stars seem to move because the Earth rotates on its axis, showing us different parts of the sky as the year progresses. In addition, as Earth revolves around the Sun, the regions of the sky that are visible to us change.

You can find your way around the sky any time of night and in any season if you use a *planisphere* or star model. This device is a wheel-shaped star chart that can be rotated and lined up with a particular time and date. In this activity, you will make a planisphere.

## Time Required

55 minutes

## Materials

- astronomy books showing constellations or access to the Internet
- scissors
- tape
- photocopy of Figure 1
- photocopy of Figure 2
- science notebook

## Procedure

1. Cut out the photocopy of Figure 1, which will serve as the frame of your planisphere. Cut along the dark line across the top of the page (the line labeled with times) and the dark oval in the center of the page.

2. Cut out the photocopy of Figure 2 along the dark outer line that encircles the names of the months. This will serve as your sky disk or wheel.

3. Notice that some of the constellations in Figure 2 are labeled, but not all of them. Use astronomy books or the Internet to determine the names of the constellations that have blanks where the names belong. Write the names on the blanks. The constellations that are missing are: Aquarius, Pegasus, Pisces, Cetus, Eridanus, Cygnus, Lyra, Hercules, Draco, Ursa Minor, Ursa Major, Cassiopeia, Cepheus, Lepus, Taurus, Orion, Canis Minor, Canis Major, Gemini, Hydra, and Canis Major.

4. Fold the cutout of Figure 1 along the three dashed lines. Tape the folds in place to form a pocket.

5. Insert the cutout of Figure 2, the sky disk, into the pocket.

6. Rotate the disk to observe how the stars and constellations move. The months at the top of the page tell you when these heavenly bodies are visible. If you want to know how the sky will look tonight at 9:00 P.M., find today's date and line it up with 9:00 P.M. The stars you see in the oval will be out tonight.

## Analysis

1. What is the purpose of a planisphere?

2. Set the star wheel so that 12:00 P.M. on the frame is pointing to December 25 on the sky disk. What are three constellations found along the southern horizon?

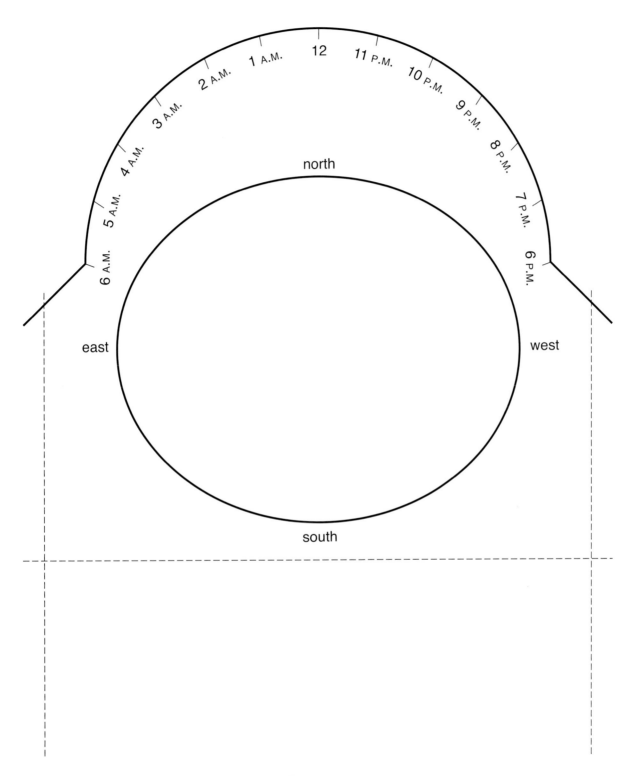

**Figure 1**

**Frame of the planisphere**

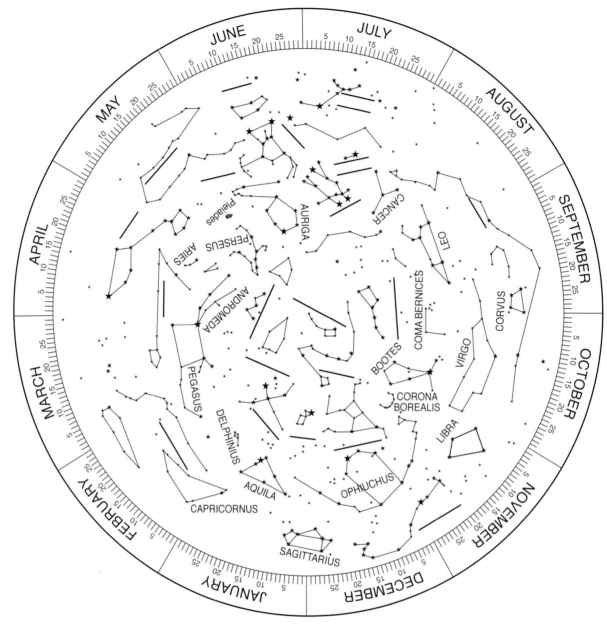

**Figure 2**

**Sky disk of the planisphere**

3. On this same date, where is the constellation Hydra?

4. Pretend that you observe the night sky every evening at 9:00 P.M. Give the month and day on which the entire constellation of Scorpius first becomes visible.

5. Remove your sky map from the pocket and find the center of the circle. (You may need to fold the map to do this.) The centermost part of the night sky is called the *zenith*. What constellation is closest to the zenith?

6. On January 9, you observe Ursa Minor at 9:00 P.M. Describe its position.

7. Describe the position of Ursa Minor on June 13 at 9:00 P.M.

8. What constellations were rising (appearing on the eastern horizon) when you were born? What constellations were at the zenith on your birthday?

## What's Going On?

By cutting out the photocopy of Figure 1, you created the framework of the planisphere. Notice that the times are written across the top of Figure 1. By inserting the photocopy of Figure 2 into the pocket of Figure 1, you have a wheel that can be rotated. To use the planisphere, rotate the inner disk or wheel to a particular time and date. In the oval opening, you will see a map of the sky that is visible on that date. Notice that the edges or horizons of the oval are labeled north, south, east, and west. Imagine that you are standing in an open field and these horizons are the edges of the sky all around you. When holding the planisphere in front of you, the horizons seem reversed. However, if you hold the planisphere above your head and read the cardinal points, they indicate the directions with which you are familiar.

You might have to practice using the planisphere. Keep in mind that the sky overhead, the celestial sphere, is perceived as a dome. The map of the sky that you are viewing is flat. Consequently, there is some distortion in the shapes and positions of constellations. Also, there is a tremendous difference in the size of the map and the size sky. To view the sky from east to west on your map, you simply move you eyes across it. But if you were outdoors looking at the sky and facing east, the western horizon would be behind you. To see it, you would have to turn around.

The planisphere you made in class is probably not perfect for your location. When you take it outdoors, you may find that a particular star rises at

9:00 P.M. instead of 10:00 P.M. as your planisphere indicated. Keep in mind that truly accurate planispheres are designed for particular latitudes. If you were reading a sky map that was made for your exact latitude, the times might be a little different. In addition, this device does not allow for daylight saving time. Despite these problems, you can use your planisphere with very little difficulty to enhance an evening of stargazing.

## Connections

To observe the southern sky, face the south and turn the planisphere so that the Southern Hemisphere on the map is at bottom. To observe the western sky, face the west and turn the device so that Western Hemisphere on the map is at the bottom. The other two sky quadrants are observed in the same way.

To find the rising time of a star, turn the wheel so that the star is touching the east, northeast, or southeast horizon. Then read dates and times at the top of the planisphere. For example, Sirius is the brightest star in Canis Major. If you adjust the planisphere so that Sirius is just appearing on the eastern edge of the oval, you see that this star rises at different times each month: between 3:00 and 5:00 A.M. in August, between 12:30 and 2:30 A.M. in September, and so on. To observe the same star when it sets, adjust the wheel so that Sirius is touching the western horizon. You can read the dates and times across the top and find out when you can view the Sirius as it sets.

As you turn the star wheel, you will notice that some stars and constellation never rise or set; they can be seen at any time. These objects are in the center of the star wheel. The centermost point of the star wheel represents the zenith, the point directly overhead. The stars that rotate around this central point are described as *circumpolar*.

## Want to Know More?

See appendix for Our Findings.

## Further Reading

Dibon-Smith, Richard. "Constellations," October 24, 2009. Available online. URL: http://www.dibonsmith.com/menu.htm. Accessed October 2, 2010. Dibon-Smith's Web page has links to information about each constellation, sky charts, and the Messier list.

Dolan, Chris. "The Constellations and Their Stars." Available online. URL: http://www.astro.wisc.edu/~dolan/constellations/. Accessed October 2, 2010. This Web site, by Chris Dolan at the University of Wisconsin at Madison, provides the names, descriptions, and pictures of all constellations.

Neave, Paul. "Neave Planetarium," 2010. Available online. URL: http://www.neave.com/planetarium/. Accessed October 2, 2010. This interactive planetarium lets you select stars and constellations of interest with a click of the mouse.

WiZiQ. "How to Use a Planisphere (Star Finder)," 2010. Available online. URL: http://www.wiziq.com/tutorial/16383-How-to-Use-a-Planisphere-Star-Finder. Accessed October 2, 2010. This slide show explains and demonstrates how to use a planisphere.

# 19. Using a Planisphere

## Topic

A planisphere can be used to locate stars and constellations in the night sky.

## Introduction

If you have done any sky watching, you know that the arrangement of stars changes over the course of an evening and from one evening to the next. Stars repeatedly rise in the east and set in the west. Of course, the stars are not really moving. The Earth is moving, and it does so in two ways: It is revolving around the Sun, continually changing the part of the universe that we can see, and the Earth is spinning on its axis. To locate heavenly bodies in this ever-changing backdrop, an amateur astronomer needs a *planisphere*, a sky map that shows a different picture of the sky for each night of the year. Figure 1 shows a simple planisphere.

Maps of the sky have been around a long time. The early astronomers in ancient Rome used them to understand the movements of stars. Babylonian, Greek, Arabian, and Persian scientists built elaborate metal devices to study the science of the changing heavens. The simplest type of model was the planisphere. Still in use, this device is made of a star map that turns around a central point. The map is housed in a frame that only reveals the portion of the sky visible at a particular date and time. By turning the map around the central point, you can mimic the changes due to Earth's rotation. In this activity, you will use a planisphere to locate, observe, and measure objects in the night sky.

### Time Required

55 minutes

### Materials

⟡   planisphere (either the one made in Experiment 18, "Making a Planisphere," or a commercially made one)

- compass
- flashlight covered with red cellophane
- pen or pencil
- science notebook

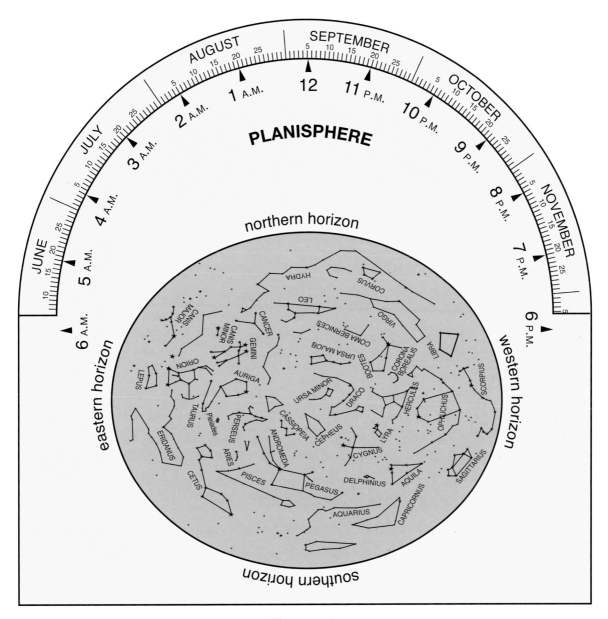

**Figure 1**

**A planisphere shows the night sky for each evening of the year.**

**Safety Note** Stay in the designated areas with your teacher. Please review and follow the safety guidelines at the beginning of this volume.

## Procedure

1. Follow your teacher to an outdoor location to observe the night sky. Take your planisphere, science notebook, flashlight covered with red cellophane, compass, and pencil or pen with you.

2. Take a few minutes to let you eyes adapt to the dark. The red light given off by your flashlight will not affect night vision.

3. Set your planisphere for today's date and time by rotating the sky map to line up the correct month, day, and time.

4. Observe the star disk. In your science notebook, write the names of 2 constellations on the planisphere near each of the following: (a) northern horizon; (b) western horizon; (c) southern horizon; and (d) eastern horizon.

5. Turn off your flashlight and look at the sky, standing so that you are facing the northern horizon. If necessary, use your compass to orient yourself to the north. Look for the two constellations you named for the northern horizon in step 4. As you find them, check them off in your notebook. If you see one or more constellations that you did not expect to find, record them your science notebook. (If you do not know their names, sketch the constellations.)

6. Repeat step 5 for the western, southern, and eastern horizons.

7. Find the *zenith*, the point in the center, on your planisphere. Put a dot at this point. What constellation is near the zenith on the planisphere? Record this constellation in your science notebook.

8. Look straight up in the sky. What constellation is almost directly overhead? Record the constellation in your science notebook.

9. Count the stars in the constellation that is overhead. Record the number in your science notebook.

10. Turn the star disk so that the constellations travel from east to west. Notice that the constellations near the center of the star disk never go below the horizons. These are known as *circumpolar constellations.* Record these in your science notebook.

11. Looking above you, find the circumpolar constellations that you recorded in your science notebook. As you find them, check them off.

12. Use your hand to estimate sky distances in degrees. Hold your index finger in front of you at arms' length. The width of your pinky is about one degree in the sky. Hold up your three middle fingers. These are about five degrees. Your fist is about 10 degrees, and your open hand is about 18 degrees (see Figure 2).

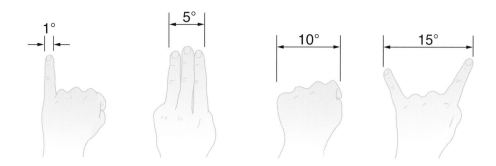

**Figure 2**

**Keep your arm fully extended in front of you when using the fingers and hand to make angular measurements.**

**13.** Estimate the distance in degrees between some stars. Find Dubhe and Megrez (see Figure 3), the top two stars in the bowl of the Big Dipper. Measure the distance in degrees using your fingers. If you found the distance to be about 10 degrees, you are measuring correctly. If not, practice until you can measure accurately.

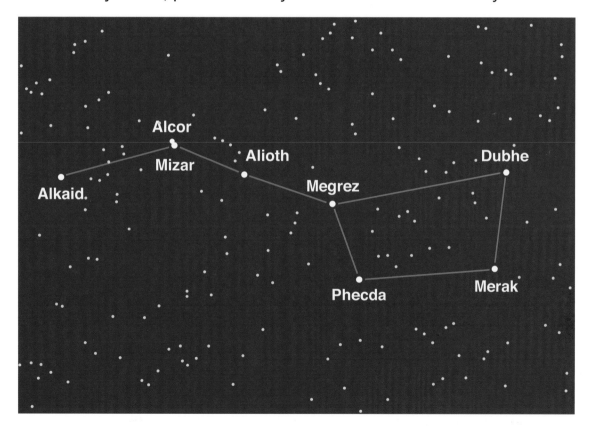

**Figure 3**

**The Big Dipper is made of the stars Dubhe, Merak, Megrez, Phecda, Alioth, Alcor and Mizar (which are very close), and Alkaid.**

**14.** Measure the distance between Dubhe and Merak, the star below Dubhe. Record your measurement in your science notebook.

**15.** The star at the end of the handle of the Little Dipper is Polaris, the North Star. How many degrees above the horizon is Polaris? Record you finding in your science notebook.

**16.** Measure the distance between Dubhe and Polaris and record the measurement in your science notebook.

## Analysis

**1.** What constellations did you see in the East? South? West? North?

**2.** What group of stars is directly overhead? How many stars could you see in this grouping?

**3.** Name the circumpolar star groups and constellations.

**4.** How long do you think it takes the circumpolar constellations to make a complete trip around Polaris?

**5.** What is the distance between Dubhe and Polaris?

**6.** What is the distance in degrees between Polaris and the horizon?

## What's Going On?

In this experiment, you used a star map to find constellations in the night sky. The constellations you located and identified that were low in the sky depended on the time of year. For example, if you were observing the sky in the winter months, November through March, you may have seen Canis Major. However, if your observations took place late spring or summer, this constellation would not visible. In the late spring, you would be able to see Scorpius, which is not visible in fall and winter.

You also located circumpolar star groups and constellations, which include Draco, Cepheus, Cassiopeia, Ursa Major, Draco, and Ursa Minor. Within the latter constellation is the well-known North Star, or Polaris. Although it is not the brightest star in the sky, Polaris is famous for its position at the zenith. Polaris marks the point around which all of the other stars appear to rotate.

Distance in the sky can be estimated by using angles. To understand the logic of the angular measurement, visualize the sky as the inside of a hollow sphere. The apparent distance between two points inside the sphere is the *angular distance*, the angle between the two points with the *vertex* at the center of the sphere. Angles measured with the vertex at the center of a sphere are expressed in degrees of arc. You estimated degrees of arc using your fingers and hand. In this case, you (or your eyes) are the vertex because you are at the center of the imaginary sphere.

## Connections

In the summer, amateur and professional sky watchers enjoy viewing the Summer Triangle, which can be seen from dusk to daybreak. The triangle, shown in Figure 4, is made up of three bright stars: Altair in the constellation Aquila, Vega in Lyra, and Deneb in Cygnus. Of the three stars, Vega is the brightest star, with a blue-white glow. If the sky is very clear, you can see a faint band of distant stars glowing between Vega and Altair. The band is the edge of the Milky Way, our galaxy.

Although named "Summer Triangle," this group of stars can be seen in different sections of the night sky all year from the northern latitudes. For regular star watchers, the grouping can serve as a calendar. In June, the triangle is found in the east in the early evening. By September, it has moved higher in the sky and is located toward the south at twilight.

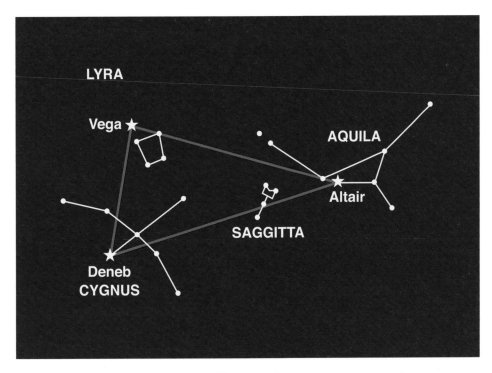

**Figure 4**

**The Summer Triangle is a bright grouping of stars that are members of three different constellations.**

The Summer Triangle is an *asterism,* a star pattern that is not a constellation. Asterisms may be made of stars from several different constellations, as is the Summer Triangle. Others are made from stars within one constellation. One of the most familiar asterisms is the Little Dipper, a distinctive grouping of stars in the constellation Ursa Minor. The Winter Hexagon is a prominent cluster of six stars in the winter sky. Each of the stars is a member of a different constellation.

### Want to Know More?

See appendix for Our Findings.

## Further Reading

Calvert, J. B. "Observing Fundamentals," March 31, 2010. "The Night Sky." Available online. URL: http://mysite.du.edu/~jcalvert/astro/obsfunds.htm. Accessed October 2, 2010. Calvert explains the essentials of observing and measuring distances in the night sky.

McClure, Bruce. "Summer Triangle: Vega, Deneb, and Altair," June 29, 2009. EarthSky. Available online. URL: http://earthsky.org/favorite-star-patterns/the-summer-triangle-roadmap-to-the-milky-way. Accessed October 2, 2010. This Web page explains how to find the Summer Triangle, a favorite of sky viewers.

Online Astronomy. "Star Gazing." Available online. URL: http://library.thinkquest.org/C005454/rstarg.html. Accessed October 2, 2010. Written by students, this Web page discusses how to get the most out of star gazing.

# 20. History of Astronomy

## Topic

Today's understanding of astronomy is built on the work of early scientists.

## Introduction

Astronomy is one of the oldest sciences. Evidence of ancient star gazing can be found across the globe. One of the best-known relics of early observations is the prehistoric monument Stonehenge, which was erected about 2500 B.C.E. in what is now England (see Figure 1). Although historians are not certain of the uses of this structure, it is generally believed to have been a ceremonial center. Several groups of stones within the center align with the positions of the Sun and Moon on certain dates.

**Figure 1**

**This reconstruction of Stonehenge shows how the monument may have appeared at one time.**

In India, historical evidence shows that astronomy has been an area of interest for centuries. Writings in *Rig Veda*, an ancient Indian book of philosophy, refer to observations of heavenly bodies around 2000 B.C.E. Indian astronomer Aryabhata (476–550 C.E.) proposed that the Sun is the center of universe, a remarkable idea considering that the Greeks did not reach this conclusion until hundreds of years later. Many accounts of astronomical study are found in Chinese history. One early theory described the Earth as the yolk of a universe shaped like an egg. Another said that the universe is infinite and contains suspended celestial bodies. As early as 1059 B.C.E., Chinese astronomers had studied and documented the heavenly body later known as Halley's comet.

Babylonians and Mesopotamians (civilizations that existed in the areas of present day Iraq and Syria) developed advanced mathematics, which they used to study the motion of the Sun and planets. They predicted the movements of heavenly bodies and developed a calendar based on these movements. Egyptian astronomers used similar techniques to create a calendar that forecast the regular flooding of the Nile River. Egyptian pyramids had features related to astronomy such has interior shafts that pointed to stars. Astronomers in ancient Egypt also relied on heavenly bodies to help the dead find their way to afterlife.

In this activity, you will research the life and work of an early astronomer and share your findings with your class.

## Time Required

three 55-minute class periods

## Materials

- ☞ access to the Internet and books on astronomers
- ☞ printer (optional)
- ☞ photocopy of grading rubric
- ☞ poster board
- ☞ colored markers
- ☞ science notebook

**Safety Note**    Please review and follow the safety guidelines at the beginning of this volume.

## Procedure, Part A

1.  Work with your lab partner to create a poster on the individual assigned to you by your teacher. This person was important in the development of the body of knowledge that is astronomy. Conduct your research on the Internet or in books on astronomy. Prepare to share your poster with the class in a short oral presentation. Your poster and oral presentation will be graded with a rubric. Be sure to look over the rubric before you begin your work. Historically important astronomers include:

    Aristotle                      Urbain Le Verrier

    Aristarchus of Samos           Clyde Tombaugh

    Eratosthenes of Cyrene         Harlow Shapley

    Claudius Ptolemy               Annie J. Cannon

    Nicolaus Copernicus            Albert Einstein

    Tycho Brahe                    Edwin Hubble

    Galileo Galilei                Hans Bethe

    Johannes Kepler                Karl Jansky

    Sir Isaac Newton               George Gamow

    Edmund Halley                  Jocelyn Bell Burnell

    William Herschel               Antony Hewish

    John Couch Adams

2.  Create a poster on the individual you were assigned that provides the following information:

    a.  *Biographical information.* When did this person live? Where did he live? What did he do for a living? Where did he study? Include all details that will make this person real to your classmates.

    b.  *Achievements.* How did this person contribute to the advancement of astronomy?

3.  Define all terms that are new to you and your classmates.

4.  On the poster, include at least three drawings or pictures that help explain this person and his contributions to astronomy.

5.  Make the poster neat, colorful, and interesting.

## Procedure, Part B

1. Present you poster to the class. Your presentation should be creative and interesting and should last about 5 minutes (min). Both partners should have a role in the presentation.

2. Answer questions from the audience.

3. When other groups present their topics, listen, take notes, and ask questions to help clarify your understanding.

## Procedure, Part C

1. Set up your poster on a table or counter so that other students can visit it.

2. Visit the poster presentations by other lab groups and take notes to help you answer the Analysis questions.

## Analysis

1. Who is the earliest astronomer in the class presentations? Who is the most recent?

2. What does the term *heliocentric universe* mean?

3. Who first proposed and explained a geocentric model of the universe?

4. What is meant by the *retrograde movement* of planets?

5. Which astronomer built an observatory with very accurate instruments that enabled him to analyze planet motion with only the naked eye observations?

6. Which astronomer analyzed Brahe's records of planetary movements over long periods of time?

7. Before Kepler, how did scientists describe the shape of planetary orbits?

8. Galileo observed that one of the planets has orbiting moons. His discovery discounted the customary idea that all objects in the universe orbit the Earth. Which planet was Galileo studying?

9. Whose law enabled Halley to calculate the orbit of a comet that was later named for him?

| Grading Rubric | | | |
|---|---|---|---|
| **Criteria** | **3** | **2** | **1** |
| When did the person live? Where did he live? What did he do for a living? Where did he study? | Poster includes all criteria. The subject is very well described. | Poster includes three of the criteria. | Poster includes two or fewer criteria. |
| How did this person contribute to the advancement of astronomy? | Several contributions to science are presented on poster. | A few contributions to science are presented on poster. | Fewer than two contributions to science are presented on poster. |
| Vocabulary | All terms were defined. | Some terms were defined. | Few terms were defined. |
| Drawings or photographs | Three or more appropriate figures were on the poster. | Two appropriate figures were on the poster. | One or no appropriate figure was on the poster. |
| Colorful, neat, interesting | The poster met all three criteria. | The poster met two criteria. | The poster met one or no criterion. |
| Presentation was shared by partners, lasted about 5 min; information on the poster was clearly explained. | Presentation met all three criteria. | Presentation met two criteria. | Presentation met one or no criterion. |
| Questions | Presenters answered all questions from the audience. | Presenters answered some questions from the audience. | Presenters answered fewer or no questions from the audience. |

**10.** Match each term to its definition.

- asteroid
- binary
- black hole
- comet
- ellipse
- galaxy
- parallax
- supernova

a. an oval-shaped path

b. a system of two stars that rotate around each other

c. small body that is larger than a meteor in orbit around the Sun

d. a star explosion that produces a tremendous amount of light

e. the seeming change in an object's position due to a change in the position of the observer

f. small, frozen mass that travels around a planet in an elliptical orbit

g. collapsed core of a star that has exhausted its fuel

h. large group of stars

## What's Going On?

After the period of early astronomy, the history of this field of science can be divided into five periods: Greek, Medieval, Renaissance, Modern, and 20th Century. Discoveries by the Greeks provided much of the groundwork for modern astronomy. Greek astronomers were philosophers who relied on logic and reason to help them understand the skies. Students of astronomy were taught that the Earth was the center of the universe. Aristarchus of Samos (310–230 B.C.E.) discovered that the Sun is much larger than Earth and proposed that the Earth revolved around the Sun. Very few scientists agreed with him. Decades after the death of Aristarchus, his ideas were still scoffed at by famous Greek philosophers such as Hipparchus (190–120 B.C.E.) and Ptolemy (ca. 87–150 C.E.).

In the Medieval period, astronomers in Persia and Arabia studied the positions of stars and the motions of planets and the Moon. Fairly accurate calculations of Earth's diameter were made. Many Europeans of the time believed that the movement of planets influenced daily life. Arabian scientists designed and built accurate observational and navigational tools that helped them use the stars to guide them during explorations.

The Renaissance period includes many of the best-known astronomers.

Nicolaus Copernicus (1473–1543), a Polish scientist, agreed with the theories of Aristarchus of Samos, whose work he expanded with the proposal that the Earth is one of several planets revolving around the Sun. Although Copernicus' logic and data made sense to many scientists of the time, his work did not fully explain the movements of the planets and the shapes of their orbits. Astronomers, including Copernicus, believed that the orbits of the planets must be circular. Figure 2 shows the Copernican model of the universe. Copernicus received strong support from Tycho Brahe (1546–1601), a great Danish scientist whose work was based on his naked-eye observations of heavenly bodies. German astronomer Johannes Kepler (1571–1630) collaborated with Brahe and analyzed his data. Kepler concluded that the planetary orbits were not circular but oval, solving a mystery that confused astronomers for decades. Italian Galileo Galilei (1564–1642) built and used telescopes for observing the planets and other heavenly bodies, and found more evidence to support Copernicus, Brahe, and Kepler.

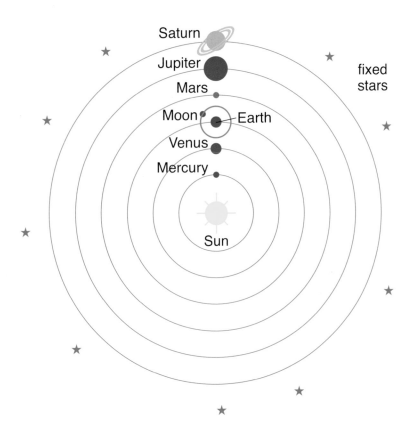

**Figure 2**

**Copernican model of the universe**

During the early years of the Modern period, a number of Englishmen made important contributions. Sir Isaac Newton (1642–1727), the most notable of the Modern astronomers, put forth his theory of universal gravitation in 1687, which was soon followed by his laws of motion. These theories helped explained why and how the planets orbit the Sun. Newton also developed mathematical models that explained the orbits of comets and the impact of Sun's gravitational pull on the Moon. He worked with Edmund Halley (1656–1742), who predicted the 1758 return of a previously observed comet , earning him the honor of having the heavenly body named after him. About the same time, John Flamsteed (1646–1719) created a catalog of stars and numbered the stars in each constellation. In 1750, Thomas Wright (1711–86) expanded knowledge on the structure of the Milky Way.

German-born British astronomer William Herschel (1738–1822) discovered Uranus in 1781. Hershel worked with his sister, Caroline Herschel (1750–1848), an excellent astronomer in her own right, and in 1802 they discovered a *binary star system*. Frenchman Charles Messier (1730–1817) organized his observations into a catalog of galaxies, nebulae, and star clusters that is still in use today. German optician Joseph von Fraunhofer (1787–1826) was interested in the nature of light. In 1814, he saw dark lines in the Sun's *spectrum* when using a device called a *diffraction grating*. His work made it possible for later scientists to develop a way to analyze the composition of stars based on the spectrum of light they emit. In 1837, another German, Wilhelm Beer (1797–1850), published the first accurate map of the Moon. Frenchman, Jean-Bernard-Léon Foucault (1819–68) demonstrated that the Earth rotates on its axis using a special pendulum.

By the 20th century, the rate of scientific discoveries in astronomy increased dramatically. New theories were built on the foundations of existing knowledge. German-born American Albert Einstein (1879–1955) developed his theories of relativity and explained that the speed of light in a vacuum is a universal constant. Dane Ejnar Hertzsprung (1873–1967) and American Henry Norris Russell (1877–1957) discovered a relationship between types of stars and their brightness. American Edwin Hubble (1889–1953) proved the existence of galaxies beyond the Milky Way and proposed that galaxies are constantly moving away from each other. British Jocelyn Bell Burnell (1943– ) discovered *pulsars*, stars that emit regular bursts of radio waves.

## Connections

In the last half of the 20th century, space exploration added a new dimension to the science of astronomy. The first satellite into space was launched in 1957 by the Soviet Union. Four years later, Russian *cosmonaut* Yuri Gagarin (1934–1968) was the first man in space. Americans Neil Armstrong (1930– ) and Edwin "Buzz" Aldrin (1930– ) landed on the Moon in 1969. The *Cosmic Background Explorer (COBE)* satellite from NASA in 1989 provided data that helped confirm the *big bang theory* on the origin of the universe. First proposed by Edwin Hubble, this theory states that about 15 billion years ago, all of the energy and matter of the universe was contained in one place. An explosion occurred that filled the universe with particles from this point. Our present universe is made up of those particles, which are still moving away from with other with incredible speed.

## Want to Know More?

See appendix for Our Findings.

## Further Reading

"Astronomy History," 1998. Astronomy Web Guide. Available online. URL: http://astronomywebguide.com/links_astronomyhistory.html. Accessed October 2, 2010. This Web site has dozens of links to pages on the people and institutions that have been important in the development of astronomy.

LaRocco, Chris, and Blair Rothstein. "The Big Bang," NASA. Available online. URL: http://www.umich.edu/~gs265/bigbang.htm. Accessed October 2, 2010. This NASA article explains the theory of the origin of the universe.

Manley, Mark. "Famous Astronomers and Astrophysicists," March 6, 2009. Available online. URL: http://cnr2.kent.edu/~manley/astronomers. html. Accessed October 2, 2010. Manley lists astronomers in alphabetical order and provides synopses of their work.

# Scope and Sequence Chart

This chart aligns the experiments in this book with some of the National Science Content Standards. (These experiments do not address every national science standard.) Please refer to your local and state content standards for additional information. As always, adult supervision is recommended and discretion should be used in selecting experiments appropriate to each age group or to individual students.

| Standard | Grades 5–8 | Grades 9–12 |
|---|---|---|
| **Physical Science** | | |
| Properties and changes of properties in matter | 3 | 3 |
| Chemical reactions | 5, 11 | 5, 11 |
| Motions and forces | | |
| Transfer of energy and interactions of energy and matter | 6, 11 | 6, 11 |
| Conservation of energy and increase in disorder | | |
| **Life Science** | | |
| Cells and structure and function in living systems | | |
| Reproduction and heredity | | |
| Regulation and behavior | | |

| Standard | Grades 5–8 | Grades 9–12 |
|---|---|---|
| Populations and ecosystems | | |
| Diversity and adaptations of organisms | | |
| Interdependence of organisms | | |
| Matter, energy, and organization in living systems | | |
| Biological evolution | | |
| **Earth Science** | | |
| Structure and energy in the Earth system | 1, 2, 6, 7, 12, 13, 14, 15, 16 | 1, 2, 6, 7, 12, 13, 14, 15, 16 |
| Geochemical cycles | 3, 4, 5, 6, 8, 9, 10, 11 | 3, 4, 5, 6, 8, 9, 10, 11 |
| Origin and evolution of the Earth system | | |
| Origin and evolution of the universe | 20 | 20 |
| Earth in the solar system | 17, 18, 19, 20 | 17, 18, 19, 20 |
| **Nature of Science** | | |
| Science in history | 20 | 20 |
| Science as an endeavor | all | all |

# Grade Level

| Title of Experiment | Grade Level |
| --- | --- |
| 1. Planimetric Maps | 6–12 |
| 2. Topographic Maps | 6–12 |
| 3. Crystal Growth and Size | 9–12 |
| 4. Erosion by Soil Type | 6–12 |
| 5. Mineral Identification | 6–12 |
| 6. Soil Color and Temperature | 6–12 |
| 7. Slope Stability | 6–12 |
| 8. Erosion on Sand Dunes | 6–12 |
| 9. Naming Rocks | 6–12 |
| 10. Rock Deformation | 6–12 |
| 11. Half-life in Rock Dating | 6–12 |
| 12. Wind Chill | 6–12 |
| 13. Relative Humidity | 6–12 |
| 14. Tracking a Hurricane | 6–12 |
| 15. Hailstone Formation | 6–12 |
| 16. Speed of Evaporation | 6–12 |
| 17. Color Filters on Telescopes | 6–9 |
| 18. Making a Planisphere | 6–12 |
| 19. Using a Planisphere | 6–12 |
| 20. History of Astronomy | 6–12 |

# Setting

The experiments are classified by materials and equipment use as follows:

- Those under SCHOOL LABORATORY involve materials and equipment found only in science laboratories. Those under SCHOOL LABORATORY must be carried out there under the supervision of the teacher or another adult.

- Those under HOME involve household or everyday materials. Some of these can be done at home, but call for supervision.

- The experiments classified under OUTDOORS may be done at school or at home, but call for supervision.

## SCHOOL LABORATORY

3. Crystal Growth and Size

5. Mineral Identification

9. Naming Rocks

15. Hailstone Formation

16. Speed of Evaporation

## HOME

2. Topographic Maps

4. Erosion by Soil Type

6. Soil Color and Temperature

7. Slope Stability

10. Rock Deformation

11. Half-life in Rock Dating

12. Wind Chill

14. Tracking a Hurricane

17. Color Filters on Telescopes

18.    Making a Planisphere

20.    History of Astronomy


## OUTDOORS

1.    Planimetric Maps

8.    Erosion on Sand Dunes

13.    Relative Humidity

19.    Using a Planisphere

# Our Findings

## 1. PLANIMETRIC MAPS

**Idea for class discussion:** Ask students to list some of the features of a good road map. Discuss the idea that there are many kinds of maps.

**Notes to the teacher:** Part B of the experiment is done outdoors. If an outdoor area is not available, you can omit this part of the experiment.

### Analysis

1. a. Boise, Idaho, 45°, 115°; b. Montgomery, Alabama, 30°, 85°; c. Raleigh, North Carolina, 35°, 80°; d. Oklahoma City, Oklahoma, 35°, 100°; e. Sacramento, California, 39°, 121°.

2. Answers will vary by location.

3. about 2,500 miles (mi) (4,100 kilometers [km])

4. about 550 mi (900 km)

5. Answers will vary based on student maps.

6. Answers will vary but will most likely include changes in distance representations, the north arrow, and symbols.

7. Legends make it possible to interpret information on maps.

## 2. TOPOGRAPHIC MAPS

**Idea for class discussion:** Show students a photograph or slide of a topographic map. Ask them what they can deduce by observing the map. Have students suggest some uses of this type of map.

### Analysis

1. 1,160 feet (ft); 1,000 ft; 1,600 ft

2. 1,080 ft; 1,140 ft

3. 1,140 ft

4. 80 ft

5. Mountain F is steepest on the north side; the contour lines are closest together on that side.

6. south

7. 163 ft

8. southeast

9. The greatest relief is shown in the upper right-hand corner where a tall peak drops from 163 ft to 109 ft.

10. Depressions are indicated with hachure marks.

11. Answers will vary based on student drawings.

12. Answers will vary based on student drawings.

## 3. CRYSTAL GROWTH AND SIZE

**Idea for class discussion:** Have students name some crystalline substances. (Some examples are quartz, salt, and diamond.) Ask them what characterizes a crystal. (Crystals are solids with an orderly arrangement of molecules.)

**Notes to the teacher:** Before class, determine whether you will use string or sticks for crystallization surface. Prepare enough surfaces for each lab group by cutting the string or sticks. Make the strings or sticks uniform lengths so that comparison of crystal growth easier.

## Analysis

1. Diagrams will vary but should resemble a sugar crystal formed step 7 of the procedure, a sample diagram is shown below.

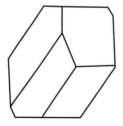

2. The sugar crystals in both jars are the shape of hexagonal prisms.

3. Answers will vary. The largest crystals will be found in a jar with a pure solution that is stored in a cool dark place with little air movement.

4. Answers will vary. Generally, pure solutions produce more crystals than those containing contaminants. Solutions left in places that are conducive to evaporation (windowsill, etc.) will have smaller, more numerous crystals.

5. Answers will vary. The weight of crystals grown in the pure solution should be greater than those grown in solutions with contaminants.

6. Answers will vary but students might suggest high concentrations of contaminant or places where there is wind or some other type of motion.

## 4. EROSION BY SOIL TYPE

**Idea for class discussion:** Ask students to describe some local erosion. Find out how much they know about the soil at the erosion site.

**Notes to the teacher:** If possible, ask some students to bring soil samples from their homes (about 6 cups of each sample). Supplement as necessary with gravel, potting soil, mulch, clay, top soil, moss, and other materials.

To extend the lesson, have students develop a procedure to find out how different types of precipitation affect erosion. Students might use cups, spray bottles, and other types of containers to distribute water over their soil.

## Analysis

1. Answers will vary depending on the types of soils the students use. Generally, small soil particles with low soil friction coefficients will erode the most.

2. Soil on a sloping surface erodes faster than similar soil on a flat surface. At approximately 41.5° to 50° of ground slope, no measures will prevent or slow soil erosion.

3. Answers will vary, but students could set up an experimental procedure based on the one used in this experiment.

4. Answers will vary. Living or dead plant matter and inorganic surface covering slows erosion.

5. Answers will vary. Students might suggest ground cover, terracing, and incorporation of soil with large particles.

## 5. MINERAL IDENTIFICATION

**Idea for class discussion:** Ask the class what kinds of tests a geologist might carry out to identify a mineral.

**Notes to the teacher:** Avoid testing rocks with clear signs of multiple mineral domains.

### Analysis

1. Results will vary. Students should support their determinations with data matching a known sample.

2. Answers will vary. If any of the minerals are magnetite raw iron, or iron-nickel the answer will be yes.

3. Answers will vary. If any of the minerals contained carbonate, the answer will be yes.

4. Answers will vary depending on the samples.

5. Answers will vary depending on the samples.

## 6. SOIL COLOR AND TEMPERATURE

**Idea for class discussion:** Ask students for some of the characteristics of different types of soil. Point out that color is a soil characteristic.

### Analysis

1. Answers will vary.

2. Answers will vary but students could list anything related to the experiment (temperature, light, moisture) except color.

3. Soils collected from different locations will have more variables than color. They will probably have different compositions and moisture contents.

4. Answers will vary.

5. Answers will vary. Students can take any of these topics and design a controlled experiment to test it.

## 7. SLOPE STABILITY

**Idea for class discussion:** Discuss landslides with the class and find out what they know about the causes.

## Analysis

1. Answers will vary depending on student results.

2. Answers will vary.

3. An experiment should only test one variable at a time to ensure that the results will be correctly interpreted.

4. Answers will vary depending on students' experimental designs.

5. Answers will vary depending on students' experimental designs.

6. Answers will vary. Students might suggest testing another variable, such as soil type or amount of moisture in soil.

## 8. EROSION ON SAND DUNES

**Idea for class discussion:** Show a picture or slide of erosion fencing on a sand dune. Ask students to explain why this fencing is needed.

## Analysis

1. Answers will vary based on expermental results.

2. Answers will vary, but the amount of erosion will have increased.

3. Answers will vary, but the amount of erosion will have increased.

4. Popsicle™ sticks slowed the amount of erosion.

5. Fabric was more effective than Popsicle™ sticks at slowing erosion.

6. Answers will vary.

7. Answers will vary, but students might point out that plants block the wind and plant roots help consolidate sand particles.

## 9. NAMING ROCKS

**Idea for class discussion:** Hold up two or three local rocks and see if students can name them. Discuss the fact that knowing something about a rock's characteristics helps one determine the rock type.

**Notes to the teacher:** Prepare rocks for each lab group to examine as follows:

a. Place these six igneous rocks in an empty egg carton: basalt, scoria, obsidian, pumice, rhyolite, and granite. Assign each rock a number and write the number on the egg carton.

b. Place these five metamorphic rocks in an empty egg carton: schist, gneiss, slate, quartzite, marble. Assign each rock a number and write the number on the egg carton.

c. Place these five sedimentary rocks in an empty egg carton: dolomite, sandstone, limestone, mudstone, shale. Write the name of each rock on the carton.

## Analysis

1. Pumice is bubbly and obsidian is smooth and glassy. Lava that forms pumice cooled slowly whereas lava forming obsidian cooled very quickly.

2. Answers will vary. Both rocks contain a lot of air bubbles, which reduces their density.

3. slate

4. Gneiss has a banded appearance.

5. shale, sandstone, and conglomerate

6. sandstone, mudstone, and conglomerate

7. Carbon-containing rocks such as dolomite and limestone produce bubbles.

## 10. ROCK DEFORMATION

**Idea for class discussion:** Show students a photograph or slide of a rock fold and ask them how this might have occurred.

## Analysis

1. a. recumbent; b. symmetrical; c. overturned; d. asymmetrical

2. Answers will vary based on student results.

3. Answers will vary. Students may have created elongated blocks of clay then compressed them slowly.

4. a. syncline; b. adjacent syncline and anticline

## 11. HALF-LIFE IN ROCK DATING

**Idea for class discussion:** Ask students to name some radioactive substances. Have them suggest a definition of *radioactive*.

## Analysis

1.  The sample "decomposed" after seven half-lives, which is 9,600 years.

2.  Because there is no such thing as half of an atom, the entire sample would be gone after another half-life had elapsed.

3.  Graphs should include the length of time on the X-axis and the number of beanium atoms on the Y-axis. The graph should have seven bars to represent the number of beanium atoms remaining in each of the samples. The first bar will be the tallest, and the last will be the shortest.

4.  Answers will vary. Generally, a sample of atoms contains stable and unstable isotopes of an element that are present in a particular ratio. Unstable isotopes of atoms decay at a predictable rate. By applying the ratio of stable to unstable isotopes, scientists can use the number of stable isotopes present to determine the number of unstable isotopes that were originally present. By comparing the original number to the amount remaining, scientists can use the length of the half-life to determine the age of the sample.

5.  70. The sample goes through three half-lives and is split in half three times.

6.  It is 3,500 years old. The sample goes through four half-lives of 875 years.

## 12. WIND CHILL

**Idea for class discussion:** Ask which is colder, a snowy day when the wind is blowing or a calm snowy day. Find out what students know about wind chill.

**Notes to the teacher:** If possible, used battery-operated fans rather than electric fans.

## Analysis

1.  Water in the container represents the body.

2.  Heat was lost fastest when the fan blew across the water.

3.  Wind speeds up the loss of heat from the body.

4.  Answers will vary. The faster the wind blows, the faster heat is lost.

5.  Answers will vary depending on student anemometer readings.

6. Answers will vary based on student results.

7. Answers will vary depending on student calculations. Differences could be due to inaccurate readings or mistakes in calculations.

## 13. RELATIVE HUMIDITY

**Idea for class discussion:** Ask students to explain how water vapor gets into the air.

## Analysis

1. Answers will vary. Evaporation is a cooling process, so evaporating water cooled the wet bulb thermometer.

2. Answers will vary based on experimental results.

3. Answers will vary. Outdoor relative humidity would be highest when the temperature is highest, usually at midday.

4. When relative humidity is high, sweat is less able to evaporate. Evaporation slows when the air is already filled with water vapor.

5. low. When the air is dry, a lot of evaporation occurs off the wet bulb, dropping the temperature of that thermometer and creating a large difference between the two instruments.

## 14. TRACKING A HURRICANE

**Idea for class discussion:** What was the most recent hurricane that students recall? Ask them to describe some events related to that hurricane.

## Analysis

1. the Bahamas

2. in southern Florida

3. a. tropical depression; b. hurricane 1; c. hurricane 1; d. hurricane 4; e. hurricane 3

4. The storm moderated and its status dropped from hurricane 3 to storm.

5. 1,007 mB; in the Bahamas

6. 902 mB; in the Gulf of Mexico

7. a. increase; b. decrease

8. As air pressure drops, wind speed increases.

9. over land (Mississippi and Tennessee)

10. 6 1/2 days; 1 more day is shown on the data table

11. Answers will vary. The paths should be very similar.

12. Answers will vary. By studying hurricane behavior, scientists can better predict the paths of future hurricanes.

## 15. HAILSTONE FORMATION

**Idea for class discussion:** Ask if any students have experienced a hailstorm. Have them describe the event and the hail. If none of your students has experienced hail, ask how they think being caught in a hailstorm would differ from being caught in a rainstorm.

## Analysis

1. Answers will vary, but the temperature was probably a little below 32 degrees Fahrenheit (°F) (0 degrees Celsius [°C]).

2. 32°F (0°C)

3. Answers will vary. The temperature in the beaker and test tube are the same. The test tube has been in the cold water bath long enough to equalize the temperatures.

4. The contents are still liquid or "not frozen."

5. Ice crystals formed. Explanations will vary, but students may say that the ice acted as nuclei around which crystals could form.

6. Answers will vary. Any particle should produce ice crystals in the test tube.

7. Answers will vary. Particles in the test tube could have served as condensation nuclei.

8. Hail formation required moisture, very cold temperatures, and the presence of condensation nuclei.

## 16. SPEED OF EVAPORATION

**Idea for class discussion:** Discuss the hydrologic cycle and the role of evaporation in this cycle.

## Analysis

1. a. increase; b. increase; c. increase

2. Answers will vary. When students were testing one experimental factor, all others should have been held constant.

3. a. High humidity will slow evaporation. b. The greater the surface area, the faster the rate of evaporation.

4. Answers will vary. Lawns should be watered at night (or near dusk and dawn) when light and heat will not aid evaporation.

5. When it is windy, because wind helps break apart hydrogen bonds at the surface of water and it removes water vapor just above water.

## 17. COLOR FILTERS ON TELESCOPES

**Idea for class discussion:** Find out from students what they know about the nature of light and see if they recognize Roy G. Biv, an acronym for the order of the colors of the rainbow—red, orange, yellow, green, blue, indigo, violet.

## Analysis

1. Answers will vary. White light includes red, orange, yellow, green, blue, indigo, and violet.

2. Answers will vary. Grass absorbs all of the colors of light except green, which it reflects to your eyes.

3. Answers will vary. Astronomers use color filters to reduce glare, increase contrast, and make some subtle features more obvious.

4. Answers will vary based on experimental results.

5. Only yellow, because yellow light is transmitted through the filter; all other colors of light are blocked.

## 18. MAKING A PLANISPHERE

**Idea for class discussion:** Find out if any students have visited a planetarium. If so, ask them to describe the experience. If not, show students a picture or slide of a planetarium show.

## Analysis

1. A planisphere helps one locate objects in the sky at different times of year.

2. Canis, Cetus Lepus, and Eridanus

3. Hydra is near the eastern horizon.

4. September 4

5. Ursa Minor

6. Answers will vary. The "handle" of the constellation is pointing down.

7. Answers will vary. The "handle" of the constellation is pointing up.

8. Answers will vary.

## 19. USING A PLANISPHERE

**Idea for class discussion:** Ask students how they would go about locating a constellation in the sky. Most will say they just look around. Point out the advantages of having a sky map.

## Analysis

1. Answers will vary depending on time of year.

2. Ursa Minor. Answers will vary. Students can most likely see seven stars.

3. Ursa Minor, Draco, Cepheus, Cassiopeia, and Ursa Major

4. Answers may vary. 24 hours

5. 25 degrees

6. 90 degrees

## 20. HISTORY OF ASTRONOMY

**Idea for class discussion:** Explain to the class why early astronomers believed that the Earth is the center of the universe.

**Notes to the teacher:** If you have a small class, you may not have enough groups to assign all of the astronomers. In that case, be sure to include the following astronomers whose work is covered in the Analysis questions: Aristotle, Bell, Brahe, Copernicus, Galileo, Halley, Kepler, Newton. A short synopsis of each astronomer is given below. Aristotle: 384–322 B.C.E. Greek philosopher and scientist. Described the five elements as fire, earth, air, water, and aether.

Aristarchus of Samos: 310–230 B.C.E. Greek astronomer who proposed that the Earth orbits the Sun, an unpopular idea at the time.

Eratosthenes of Cyrene: 276–194 B.C.E. Greek mathematician who first measured the circumference of Earth.

Claudius Ptolemy: 90–ca.168 C.E. Roman philosopher who supported the idea of a geocentric universe.

Copernicus: 1473–1543. Polish scientist who postulated that Earth is one of several planets orbiting the Sun.

Tycho Brahe: 1546–1601. Danish astronomer who catalogued very accurate observations of the movements of stars and planets. The first astronomer to observe and gather data on a supernova.

Galileo Galilei: 1564–1642. Italian physicist, mathematician, astronomer, and philosopher. Improved the telescope. In 1610, supported the ideas of Copernicus, despite the general support for geocentric theory. Discovered three of Jupiter's four moons. Described the phases of Venus. Observed and charted the movement of sunspots. Observed and described the Moon's surface. Described theories of uniform motion and general relativity.

Johannes Kepler: 1571–1630. German mathematician, astronomer, and astrologer. Worked with Tycho Brahe on observations of Mars. Wrote the laws of planetary motion.

Sir Isaac Newton: 1642–1727. English physicist, mathematician, and astronomer. Discovered gravity and wrote the three laws of motion. Experimented with light and improved telescopes.

Edmund Halley: 1656–1742. English astronomer, geophysicist, mathematician, and meteorologist. Calculated orbit and eponymous of Halley's comet.

William Herschel: 1738–1822. British astronomer and composer. Discovered Uranus and infrared radiation. Built more than 400 telescopes, including the largest one of the day, with focal length of 40 feet (ft) (12 meters [m]).

John Couch Adams: 1819–92. British mathematician and astronomer. Predicted the presence of Neptune from irregularities in the orbit of Uranus.

Urbain Le Verrier: 1811–77. French mathematician. Using mathematical calculations, predicted the existence and size of Neptune.

Clyde Tombaugh: 1906–97. American astronomer. Discovered Pluto and many asteroids.

Harlow Shapley: 1885–1972. American astronomer. Conducted research in determining the distances to globular clusters. Found that the Milky Way was much larger than originally believed.

Annie J. Cannon: 1863–1941. American astronomer. One of the first to classify stars based on their temperatures.

Albert Einstein: 1879–1955. German-born American physicist. Developed theories of special and general relativity and identified the speed of light in a vacuum as a constant.

Edwin Hubble: 1889–1953. American astronomer. Found that galaxies are moving away from each other.

Hans Bethe: 1906–2005. German-born American physicist. Proposed that the energy in stars comes from nuclear reactions in which hydrogen is converted into helium.

Karl Jansky: 1905–50. American physicist and engineer. Discovered that radio waves are emitted by the Milky Way.

George Gamov: 1904–68. Russian-born American physicist. Proposed how levels of hydrogen and helium in the universe could have resulted from the big bang theory.

Jocelyn Bell Burnell: 1943– . British astrophysicist. Worked with Hewish and developed a radio telescope that enabled her to discover the first neutron star.

Anthony Hewish: 1924– . British astrophysicist. Worked with Burnell and developed a radio telescope that enabled her to discover the first neutron star.

## Analysis

1. Aristotle; Jocelyn Bell
2. Sun-centered
3. Copernicus
4. *Retrograde* refers to an apparent backward movement of planets.
5. Tycho Brahe
6. Kepler

7. Planetary orbits were described as circular for about 2,000 years before Kepler's calculations showing that they are elliptical.

8. Jupiter

9. Newton's law of universal gravitation

10. a. ellipse; b. binary; c. asteroid; d. supernova; e. parallax; f. comet; g. black hole; h. galaxy

# Glossary

**abiotic**   relating to the nonliving factors in the environment

**albedo**   amount of sunlight reflected from a surface

**alpha particle**   positively charged particle emitted through radioactive decay

**angle of incidence**   the angle made by light when it strikes a surface

**angular distance**   angular separation between two objects as perceived by an viewer

**anticline**   fold in rock layers in the shape of an inverted *U*

**asterism**   pattern of stars in the night sky that is not a constellation

**asteroids**   masses of metallic rock orbiting the Sun that are larger than meteors but smaller than planets

**atomic number**   number of protons in the nucleus of an atom

**axial plane**   the imaginary line that splits a fold into two parts

**beta particle**   high-speed electron emitted through radioactive decay

**big bang theory**   the idea that the universe began from a single point, or singularity, that expanded rapidly and is still expanding

**binary**   two objects in space that are close together and orbit around a center of mass

**biotic**   relating to the living factors in the environment

**black hole**   region of space with a very strong gravitational field from which nothing, not even light, can escape

**carbonate**   compound that contains carbon and oxygen such as calcium carbonate, $CaCO_3$

**cartography**   the study of making charts and maps

**celestial sphere**   an imaginary sphere that is the backdrop for all objects in space

**chroma**   the strength of a color, the purity of the hue

**circumpolar constellations**   group of constellations that appear to rotate around Polaris and that are visible through all seasons

**climate**   long-term weather pattern in a region

**cohesion**   attraction of like molecules

**color filter**   sheet of colored film that is used to block some colors and allow others to be transmitted

**comet**   small, icy body that travels around the Sun in an elliptical orbit; near the Sun, it shows a fuzzy coma and a long tail

**condensation particle**   tiny particle such as dust or ice on which water vapor condenses

**conduction**   transfer of heat in a substance from one molecule to the next

**constellation**   defined area of the celestial sphere; historically, a pattern formed by stars

**contour line**   line on a topographic map showing areas of equal elevation

**contrast**   difference in the properties of an image that makes it distinguishable from its background

**Coriolis effect**   deflection of objects from their straight line course due to the rotation of Earth on its axis

**cosmonaut**   Russian or Soviet pilot trained for space travel

**crepuscular**   active at twilight or dawn when light is low

**crust**   outermost solid layer of Earth

**crystal**   solid whose basic particles are arranged in a repeating pattern

**crystal diffraction**   the deflection or bending of light waves as they move through a crystal

**cumulonimbus cloud**   tall, dense cloud associated with thunderstorms

**diffraction grating**   device made of a surface containing many parallel grooves that split a beam of white light into its component wavelengths

**disaccharide**   a sugar molecule made up of two subunits

**downdraft**   downward-moving current of air

**electromagnetic spectrum**   entire range of radiation that travels through space, from long wavelength, low-frequency radio waves to short wavelength, high-frequency gamma rays

**electron capture**   type of radioactive decay in which an orbital electron is captured and unites with the nucleus

**elevation**   height of an object or place above a fixed reference point, such as sea level

**ellipse**   shape of an orbit that looks like a oval or a flattened circle

**erosion**   the wearing away of the Earth's surface by wind, water, or chemical reactions

**evapotranspiration**   the sum of water returned to the atmosphere by transpiration from plants and evaporation from the Earth's surface

**eye wall**   an area of fast-moving wind surrounding the eye of a storm

**fault**   crack or fracture in the Earth's crust resulting in a shifting of the rock on one side

**festoon**   finger-shaped belt of clouds on Jupiter's surface

**fold**   bend in one or multiple layers of rock

**foliation**   rock structure in which minerals are arranged in flattened layers

**friction**   force between surfaces that resists movement

**frostbite**   damage to tissues by freezing

**galaxy**   large collection of stars in a gravitationally bound system

**gamma particle**   high-energy electromagnetic radiation released during radioactive decay

**geologist**   scientist who studies the materials that make up the Earth

**glare**   excessive brightness, either direct or reflected, that interferes with viewing

**global warming**   increase in Earth's surface temperature due to thickening of a zone of atmospheric greenhouse gases

**graupel**   small pellets formed when snowflakes are coated with supercooled droplets of water that freeze on contact

**greenhouse gases**   layer of carbon dioxide and other gases in the atmosphere that trap heat near the Earth's surface

**hachured**   on a topographic map, marked with small lines to represent a depression

**hail**   solid precipitation formed of irregularly shaped pieces of ice that is created when droplets of water are repeatedly carried aloft by strong updrafts

**half-life**   the time it takes for one-half of the atoms of a radioactive material to decay

**heliocentric universe**   theory that the Earth and other planets revolve around the Sun

**hue**   the color of an object due to the wavelengths of light reflected from it

**humidity**   amount of water vapor in the air

**hurricane**   rotating storm over the ocean that has sustained wind speeds of 74 miles (mi) per hour (119 kilometers [k] per hour)

**hydrogen bond**   weak bond that forms between the slight, opposite charges on molecules

**hydrologic cycle**   continuous movement of water on Earth that includes evaporation from surfaces; condensation in the atmosphere; precipitation; absorption by soil and plants; and runoff into streams, rivers, lakes, and the ocean.

**hygrometer**   instrument used to measure relative humidity

**hypothermia**   condition in which the body temperature drops below normal

**igneous rock**   rock formed when molten magma or lava cools

**infrared energy**   invisible electromagnetic waves that are slightly long than red light

**ion**   atom or molecule that is electrically charged

**isotope**   one of two or more atoms with the same number of protons but different numbers of neutrons

**landform**   any distinct geological feature on Earth's surface, such as a hill or cave

**landslide**   movement of a mass of dirt, rocks, and mud down a slope

**latent heat**   thermal energy released or absorbed when a substance changes phase

**latitude**   angular distance on Earth north or south of the equator

**law of conservation of energy**   principle that the total amount of energy in a system remains constant because energy cannot be created or destroyed

**legend**   on a map, a brief description of symbols

**lepton**   subatomic particle that participates in weak interactions with other particles

**longitude**   angular distance on Earth east or west of the prime meridian

**luster**   appearance of the surface of a mineral in relation to  the way light interacts with it

**mantle**   thick, viscous layer located between the crust and the core that makes up two-thirds of the Earth's mass

**map**   representation of an area showing features and their positions to scale

**maria**   dark, smooth regions on the surface of planets or moons

**mass number**   sum of protons and neutrons in the nucleus of an atom

**matrix**   region of the soil having the dominant soil color

**metamorphic rock**   rock that has been changed from its original form by heat or pressure

**meteorologist**   scientist who studies the atmospheric processes that cause weather

**mineral**   naturally occurring, solid inorganic substance that has a definite chemical makeup

**Munsell color system**   scheme for classifying color based on its hue, value, and chroma

**nebula**   cloud of gas and dust in space

**neutrino**   subatomic particle with no mass and no charge that participates in weak interactions with other particles

**nitrification**   the process of changing ammonia to nitrite or nitrate ions

**nocturnal**   active during the night

**parallax**   apparent displacement of an object when viewed from two different positions

**phase**   state of matter (solid, liquid, or gas)

**pioneer plants**   small, drought-tolerant plants that are the first to appear on new landforms

**planimetric map**   map that shows the horizontal features of an area

**planisphere**   star chart of the celestial sphere that can be adjusted so that the stars at a particular time and date appear in a window

**polar**   having a positive end and a negative end

**polyhedron**   three-dimensional solid with many flat features and straight edges

**positron emission**   radioactive decay in which a proton is changed to a neutron, positron, and neutrino

**precipitate**   the falling to Earth of any form of water such as rain, sleet, snow, or hail; process in which a solid substance falls out of solution

**precipitation**   any product of the condensation of atmospheric water vapor (rain, snow, sleet, or hail) that fall to Earth

**prime meridian**   line of 0° longitude that joins the north and south poles and passes through Greenwich, England

**prism**   triangular optical device that can diffract light into its colors

**protein receptor**   structure on a cell membrane that can bind to a protein

**psychrometer**   type of hygrometer made of a dry-bulb and a wet-bulb thermometer

**quark**   one of the most elementary forms of matter and a constituent of protons and neutrons

**radioactive decay**   process in which unstable nuclei break down, emitting particles and radiation, to a more stable form

**radiometric dating**   method used to find the age of materials based on a comparison of the abundance of a radioactive isotope and its decay product(s)

**relative humidity**   ratio of the amount of water vapor in the air to the amount of water vapor the air could hold

**relief**   the differences in elevation within an area of the Earth's surface, as shown on a map

**retrograde movement**   motion that is in the opposite direction to usual motion

**Richter scale**   unit of measure for quantifying the amplitude of an earthquake

**rock**   solid, naturally occurring mixture of minerals

**saltation**   type of particle transport by wind or water in which particles leap along a surface

**saltwort**   low-growing shrub found in coastal areas

**sand dune**   mound of sand particles deposited by wind

**saturation point**   the point at which no more solute can be dissolved in a solution, whether liquid or gaseous

**scale**   ratio between the size of something and the size of its representation

**sedimentary rock** rock made from particles that are deposited and cemented together

**shear strength** resistance to movement down a slope

**shear stress** force that moves one part of a material sideways past another part

**silt** soil made up of particles intermediate in size between sand and clay

**soil** the loose mixture of minerals and organic matter on Earth's surface

**solar noon** time at which the Sun is at the highest point in the sky

**stereoscope** binocular scope for viewing photographs in three dimensions

**supercool** to lower the temperature of a liquid below its freezing point without a change in phase, as from water to ice

**supernova** extremely bright star explosion

**surface tension** property at the surface of a liquid due to intermolecular forces within the liquid

**syncline** fold in rock layers in the shape of a *U*

**tectonic plates** large sections of the Earth's crust that move very slowly on top of the mantle

**tessellate** to fit together, with no overlapping edges or gaps

**topographic map** map that shows changes in elevation along with natural and cultural features

**topsoil** the upper layer of soil, having the highest percentage of organic matter

**tropical depression** area of atmospheric circulation around an area of low pressure producing winds up to 39 miles (mi) per hour (61 kilometers [km] per hour); precursor to a hurricane

**unit cell** the smallest, orderly arrangement of particles in a crystal

**updraft** upward moving current of air

**value** the lightness or darkness of a color compared to white; the color's brightness

**variable** part of a procedure that varies during an experiment

**vertex** point at the corner of a geometric shape

**weathering** the break down of rocks on Earth's surface by chemical or physical forces

**wind chill factor** the apparent temperature felt on skin due to cooling and wind

**wind shear** change in wind speed and direction over a relatively short distance in the atmosphere

# Internet Resources

The World Wide Web is an invaluable source of information for students, teachers, and parents. The following list is intended to help you get started exploring educational sites that relate to the book. It is just a sample of the Web material that is available to you. All of these sites were accessible as of October 2010.

## Educational Resources

Anthoni, J. Floor. "Soil: Dependence—How society depends on soil," 2000. Available online. URL: http://www.seafriends.org.nz/enviro/soil/depend.htm. Accessed October 2, 2010. Anthoni's interesting Web page discusses humans in the food chain and contrasts the positions of vegetarians and meat eaters.

Bradley, David. "The properties of water." Watercourse. Available online. URL: http://www.waterconservators.org/prop.html. Accessed October 2, 2010. Bradley explains why water creates hydrogen bonds and how these bonds affect its chemical characteristics in this article.

Environmental Protection Agency. Available online. URL: http://www.epa.gov/. Accessed October 2, 2010. The EPA Web site has links to all topics relating to the environment, including loss of ozone in the stratosphere.

Favis-Mortlock, David. Soil Erosion Site. February 12, 2008. Available online. URL: http://soilerosion.net/. Accessed October 2, 2010. This Web site is a gateway for information on soil erosion that can be used by students or specialists. The site provides links to photos and videos, as well as organizations and meeting on topics related to erosion.

Fichter, Lynn. "Minerals," 2000. Available online. URL: http://csmres.jmu.edu/geollab/fichter/Minerals/index.html. Accessed October 2, 2010. Fichter provides alphabetical lists of minerals with links to their properties.

Gardiner, Lisa. "Earth's Oceans," Windows to the Universe, September 31, 2008. Available online. URL: http://www.windows.ucar.edu/tour/link=/earth/Water/ocean.html. Accessed October 2, 2010. Gardiner's Web site discusses waves, currents, coral reefs, ocean life, and other topics related to marine science.

Garrigan, Mary. "Massive Hail Stones Fall in Tiny South Dakota Town, Challenge U.S. Record," July 27, 2010. *Rapid City Journal*. Available online. URL: http://www.rapidcityjournal.com/news/article_2f011372-9902-11df-9314-001cc4c002e0.html. Accessed October 2, 2010. Garrigan describes a hail storm that produced stones 18.5 inches (in) (47 centimeters [cm]) in diameter.

Horstmeyer, Steven L. "Relative Humidity . . . Relative to What? The Dew Point Temperature. . . a Better Approach," 2008. Available online. URL: http://www.shorstmeyer.com/wxfaqs/humidity/humidity.html. Accessed October 2, 2010. Meteorologist Horstmeyer explains some of the misconceptions on the topic of relative humidity in this aritcle.

International Union of Crystallography. Available online. URL: http://www.iucr.org/iucr. Accessed October 2, 2010. This Web site has links to dozens of articles on advanced topics in crystallography.

Jessey, Dave, and Don Tarman. "Mineral Identification: The Beauty of Nature." Project ALERT. Available online. URL: http://geology.csupomona.edu/alert/mineral/minerals.htm. Accessed October 2, 2010. Jessey and Tarman, professors of geology at Cal Poly-Pomona, explain how the physical properties of minerals can help in mineral identification.

KidsAstronomy.com, 2010. Available online. URL: http://www.kidsastronomy.com/. Accessed October 2, 2010. This colorful, easy-to-read Web site provides information on the solar system as well as deep-space objects.

Krantz, David, and Brad Kifferstein. "Water Pollution and Society." Available online. URL: http://www.umich.edu/~gs265/society/waterpollution.htm. Accessed October 2, 2010. In this article, the authors describe sources of water pollution and discuss some of the techniques used to purify water.

"Map Projections, Grids, Image Rectification, Planimetric Mapping." Mississippi State University, College of Forest Resources. Available online. URL: http://www.cfr.msstate.edu/students/forestrypages/fd/fo4313/topic11.pdf. Accessed October 2, 2010. This detailed article explains a map projection, a mapping system that takes into account the Earth's curvature.

Mineralogy 4 Kids. "Mineral Identification." Mineralogy Society of America. Available online. URL: http://www.minsocam.org/MSA/K12/properties/minid/mineralid.html. Accessed October 2, 2010. This interactive Web site helps students identify minerals by their physical characteristics.

NASA. "Ozone Hole Watch," March 14, 2010. Available online. URL: http://ozonewatch.gsfc.nasa.gov/. Accessed October 2, 2010. This Web page provides daily updates on the status of the ozone hole.

National Oceanic & Atmospheric Administration (NOAA). "Hurricane Katrina—Most Destructive Hurricane Ever to Strike the U.S.," February 12, 2007. Available online. URL: http://www.katrina.noaa.gov/. Accessed October 2, 2010. This comprehensive Web site provides photographs of the hurricane and aftermath, aerial images, and maps.

Nave, C. R. "Relative Humidity," 2005. Hyperphysics. Available online. URL: http://hyperphysics.phy-astr.gsu.edu/hbase/kinetic/relhum.html. Accessed October 2, 2010. Nave of Georgia State University provides links to pages on dozens of topics related to astronomy and physics, including this one on relative humidity.

Nemiroff, Robert, and Jerry Bonnell. "Astronomy Picture of the Day." Available online. URL: http://antwrp.gsfc.nasa.gov/apod/astropix.html. Accessed October 2, 2010. Each day, this Web site features a photograph of some part of the universe along with an explanation written by an astronomer.

Stern, David P. *From Stargazers to Starships*, January 21, 2008. Available online. URL: http://www.phy6.org/stargaze/Sintro.htm. Accessed October 2, 2010. Stern provides an online text book in astronomy for beginners.

Strickler, Mike. "GeoMania." Available online. URL: http://jersey.uoregon.edu/~mstrick/index.html. Accessed October 2, 2010. Strickler provides lecture notes on various topics in geology along with guides for studying rocks and minerals on this Web site.

USGS Maps. April 13, 2005. Available online. URL: http://egsc.usgs.gov/isb/pubs/booklets/usgsmaps/usgsmaps.html. Accessed October 2, 2010. This Web site, maintained by the U.S. Department of the Interior and the U.S. Geological Survey, provides maps of the United States and its resources.

Weather Central. Available online. URL: http://www.weathercentral.com/weather/maps/us/humidity.html. Accessed October 2, 2010. This Web site provides up-to-date weather information, including a national map of relative humidity.

# Periodic Table of Elements

Key:

| | |
|---|---|
| 1 | atomic number |
| H | symbol |
| 1.008 | atomic weight |

Numbers in parentheses are the atomic mass numbers of radioactive isotopes.

| 1 | 2 | 3 | 4 | 5 | 6 | 7 | 8 | 9 | 10 | 11 | 12 | 13 | 14 | 15 | 16 | 17 | 18 |
|---|---|---|---|---|---|---|---|---|---|---|---|---|---|---|---|---|---|
| 1<br>H<br>1.008 | | | | | | | | | | | | | | | | | 2<br>He<br>4.003 |
| 3<br>Li<br>6.941 | 4<br>Be<br>9.012 | | | | | | | | | | | 5<br>B<br>10.81 | 6<br>C<br>12.01 | 7<br>N<br>14.01 | 8<br>O<br>16.00 | 9<br>F<br>19.00 | 10<br>Ne<br>20.18 |
| 11<br>Na<br>22.99 | 12<br>Mg<br>24.31 | | | | | | | | | | | 13<br>Al<br>26.98 | 14<br>Si<br>28.09 | 15<br>P<br>30.97 | 16<br>S<br>32.07 | 17<br>Cl<br>35.45 | 18<br>Ar<br>39.95 |
| 19<br>K<br>39.10 | 20<br>Ca<br>40.08 | 21<br>Sc<br>44.96 | 22<br>Ti<br>47.88 | 23<br>V<br>50.94 | 24<br>Cr<br>52.00 | 25<br>Mn<br>54.94 | 26<br>Fe<br>55.85 | 27<br>Co<br>58.93 | 28<br>Ni<br>58.69 | 29<br>Cu<br>63.55 | 30<br>Zn<br>65.39 | 31<br>Ga<br>69.72 | 32<br>Ge<br>72.59 | 33<br>As<br>74.92 | 34<br>Se<br>78.96 | 35<br>Br<br>79.90 | 36<br>Kr<br>83.80 |
| 37<br>Rb<br>85.47 | 38<br>Sr<br>87.62 | 39<br>Y<br>88.91 | 40<br>Zr<br>91.22 | 41<br>Nb<br>92.91 | 42<br>Mo<br>95.94 | 43<br>Tc<br>(98) | 44<br>Ru<br>101.1 | 45<br>Rh<br>102.9 | 46<br>Pd<br>106.4 | 47<br>Ag<br>107.9 | 48<br>Cd<br>112.4 | 49<br>In<br>114.8 | 50<br>Sn<br>118.7 | 51<br>Sb<br>121.8 | 52<br>Te<br>127.6 | 53<br>I<br>126.9 | 54<br>Xe<br>131.3 |
| 55<br>Cs<br>132.9 | 56<br>Ba<br>137.3 | 57-71* | 72<br>Hf<br>178.5 | 73<br>Ta<br>180.9 | 74<br>W<br>183.9 | 75<br>Re<br>186.2 | 76<br>Os<br>190.2 | 77<br>Ir<br>192.2 | 78<br>Pt<br>195.1 | 79<br>Au<br>197.0 | 80<br>Hg<br>200.6 | 81<br>Tl<br>204.4 | 82<br>Pb<br>207.2 | 83<br>Bi<br>209.0 | 84<br>Po<br>(210) | 85<br>At<br>(210) | 86<br>Rn<br>(222) |
| 87<br>Fr<br>(223) | 88<br>Ra<br>(226) | 89-103‡ | 104<br>Rf<br>(261) | 105<br>Db<br>(262) | 106<br>Sg<br>(263) | 107<br>Bh<br>(262) | 108<br>Hs<br>(265) | 109<br>Mt<br>(266) | 110<br>Ds<br>(271) | 111<br>Rg<br>(272) | 112<br>Uub<br>(285) | 113<br>Uut<br>(284) | 114<br>Uuq<br>(285) | 115<br>Uup<br>(288) | 116<br>Uuh<br>(292) | | 118<br>Uuo<br>(294) |

| *lanthanide series | 57<br>La<br>138.9 | 58<br>Ce<br>140.1 | 59<br>Pr<br>140.9 | 60<br>Nd<br>144.2 | 61<br>Pm<br>(145) | 62<br>Sm<br>150.4 | 63<br>Eu<br>152.0 | 64<br>Gd<br>157.3 | 65<br>Tb<br>158.9 | 66<br>Dy<br>162.5 | 67<br>Ho<br>164.9 | 68<br>Er<br>167.3 | 69<br>Tm<br>168.9 | 70<br>Yb<br>173.0 | 71<br>Lu<br>175.0 |
|---|---|---|---|---|---|---|---|---|---|---|---|---|---|---|---|
| ‡actinide series | 89<br>Ac<br>(227) | 90<br>Th<br>232.0 | 91<br>Pa<br>231.0 | 92<br>U<br>238.0 | 93<br>Np<br>(237) | 94<br>Pu<br>(244) | 95<br>Am<br>(243) | 96<br>Cm<br>(247) | 97<br>Bk<br>(247) | 98<br>Cf<br>(251) | 99<br>Es<br>(252) | 100<br>Fm<br>(257) | 101<br>Md<br>(258) | 102<br>No<br>(259) | 103<br>Lr<br>(260) |

# Index

## A

Advanced Spaceborne Thermal Emission and Reflection Radiometer (Aster) 12, 13
Aldrin, Edwin "Buzz" 141
angle of incidence 34, 35
angular distance 130
anticline 62, 64, 65, 68
Aristarchus of Samos 135, 138
Aristotle 135
arrowheads 27
Aryabhata 133
Atlantic basin 93
Aurora, Nebraska 103

## B

basalt 57, 58, 60
beaches 52
Beer, Wilhelm 140
Beichuan, China 48
beta decay 73, 75
beta particle 74
Bethe, Hans 135
big bang theory 141
Brahe, Tycho 135, 136, 139
Burnell, Jocelyn Bell 135, 140

## C

Cannon, Annie J 135
cartography 6, 12
climate 110
coal 28
cohesion 42, 47
color filters 113–116, 118
comets 28
compressive stress 62, 63
condensation particle 102
conduction 77

conglomerate 59
constellations 119, 120, 122-124, 126, 129–132
contour line 9–11
convection 77
Copernicus, Nicolaus 135, 139
coral reefs 28
Coriolis effect 95–97
Crab nebula 113
crust 28, 62, 68
crystal 14, 15, 17–19, 27, 57, 58
cumulonimbus clouds 99, 103
cyanobacteria 28

## D

deforestation 24
dew 89
dew point 88, 89
Dhahran, Saudi Arabia 89
diffraction 19
diffraction grating 140
dolomite 59
dust bowl 24

## E

earthquakes 47
ecosystem 34, 53
Einstein, Albert 135, 140
electromagnetic spectrum 13, 116, 117
electron capture 74
embryo dunes 52
equator 1, 35, 95
Eratosthenes of Cyrene 6
erosion 21, 23–25, 38, 42, 49, 52, 60, 65
evapotranspiration 106

## F

Flamsteed, John 140
fossil fuel 68, 110
fossils 70–72
Foucault, Jean Bernard Léon 140
Fraunhofer, Joseph Von 140
friction 42
frictional forces 47
frostbite 82

## G

gabbro 60
Gagarin, Yuri 141
Galileo Galilei 135, 136, 139
gamma particle 75
Gamow, George 135
geologist 27, 28
global positioning system 1
global warming 110, 111
gneiss 57-59
granite 57, 58
graupel 100
Great Red Spot 118
greenhouse gases 110, 111
ground covers 21
groundwater 68, 105, 106
Gulf of Mexico 92, 93

## H

hailstones 99–104
Haiti 24
half-life 70, 71, 73
Halley, Edmund 135, 136, 140
Halley's comet 134
heat index 89
Herschel, Caroline 140
Herschel, William 135, 140
Hertzspring, Ejnar 140

Hewish, Antony 135
Hipparchus 138
Hubble, Edwin 135, 140, 141
hurricane 92–97
Hurricane Katrina 92–94, 96
hydrogen bonds 106
hydrologic cycle 105
hygrometer 84
hypothermia 82

**I**

igneous rocks 55–58, 60
infrared camera 77
infrared energy 38
isotonic stress 62, 63
isotopes 70, 71, 73

**J**

Jansky, Karl 135
Jupiter 113, 118

**K**

Kepler, Johannes 135, 136, 139
kinetic energy 110

**L**

landslides 24, 47, 48
latent heat 91, 106
latitude 1-3, 5, 93–96, 123
lattice system 14
lava 60
law of conservation of energy 38
LeVerrier, Urbain 135
lepton 75
Leyte Island, Philippines 47
limestone 28, 59
longitude 1–3, 5, 93, 94, 96

**M**

mantle 28
marble 57–59
Mars 118
matrix 39
Messier, Charles 140

metamorphic rocks 55–60
meteorites 31
meteorologists 91, 95, 103
meteors 28
Milky Way 131, 140
minerals 14, 21, 25, 27–32, 55, 68
Mohs, Frederick 31
Mohs Hardness Scale 29–31
Moon 117
mudstone 59
Munsell color system 39

**N**

NASA 12
natural gas 32, 68,69
neutrinos 75
Newton, Sir Isaac 135, 140
nitrification 34

**O**

obsidian 57, 58
oil 32, 68, 69

**P**

photosynthesis 28
pioneer plants 53
planimetric map 1, 2
planisphere 119, 120, 123, 124, 126–128
polar 47, 106
Polaris 130
positron emission 74
precipitation 84, 91, 99, 105, 106, 110
prime meridian 2, 93
protein receptor 19
psychrometer 84, 86, 88
Ptolemy, Claudius 135, 138
pumice 57, 58

**Q**

quarks 75
quartz 31, 32
quartzite 57–59

**R**

radioactive decay 28, 70, 71
radiometric dating 70
relative humidity 84, 87-89
rhyolite 57, 58
Richter scale 48
Rig Veda 133
rock 21, 23, 24, 27, 29–31, 55–60, 62, 63, 68,70, 71
rock cycle 59, 60
Russel, Henry Norris 140

**S**

Saffir-Simpson scale 95, 97
saltation 49
sand dunes 49, 50, 52, 53
sandstone 59
scavengers 53
schist 57–59
scoria 57, 58
sea oats 52
sedimentary rocks 55, 56, 58-60
seed germination 34
shale 59
shear strength 42
shear stress 42, 62, 63
slate 57, 59
soil 21–24, 34–40, 42, 43, 45, 47
Solomon, Susan 110
stereoscope 12
Stone Age 27
Stonehenge 133
subsoil 39, 40
Summer Triangle 131, 132
surface horizons 39, 40
surface tension 47
sweat 88
syncline 62, 64, 65, 68, 69

**T**

tectonic plates 60
telescopes 113, 117, 139
tensile stress 62, 63
Terra 12

Tombaugh, Clyde  135
topographic map  8, 9, 12, 13
top soil  24, 25
tropical depression  95–97
tropical storm  95–97

**V**

volcano  47, 59, 60

**W**

Waldseemüller, Martin  6
wavelength  116, 117
weather  110
wind chill factor  78, 80, 82
wind shear  91
Wright, Thomas  140

**X**

X-ray crystallography  019